JAPANESE COOKING

Pure & Simple

JAPANESE COOKING

Pure & Simple

Consultant
David Scott

Exeter Books

NEW YORK

やさい料理

Editor: *Julia Canning*
Designer: *Johnny Pau*
Production *Richard Churchill*

First published in USA 1986 by Exeter Books
Reprinted 1987
Distributed by Bookthrift
Exeter is a trademark of Bookthrift Marketing, Inc.
Bookthrift is a registered trademark of
Bookthrift Marketing
New York, New York

ISBN 0-671-08308-2

Printed and bound in Barcelona, Spain by Cronión, S.A.

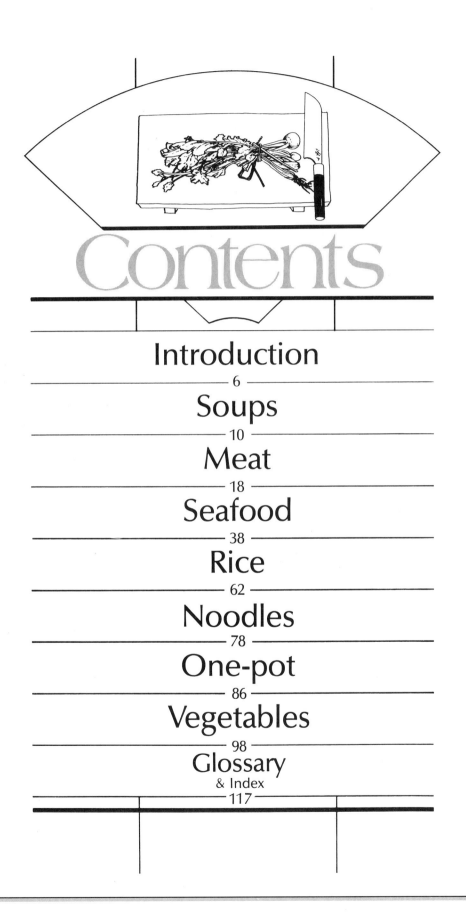

Contents

Introduction

To the Japanese, food represents much more than the pleasure of good eating. It is presented in a manner that is intended to inspire not only the senses but also the spirit.

The creation of each dish starts with the selection of only the freshest and best quality ingredients, with a spiritual awareness of each season and the food it offers. The prepared food is always decoratively arranged on dishes which have also been carefully chosen for their visual beauty.

For the Western cook, such concern can be inspiring, but the real pleasure of Japanese food perhaps comes more from the new taste experiences it offers. Japanese cooking is also appealing for its simple and quick cooking methods—ingredients retain their natural goodness and flavors.

The Japanese meal

The selection of food for a Japanese meal is based as much on its visual appeal and aesthetic quality as it is on the variety of tastes, textures and colors.

A balanced meal depends primarily on serving a selection of dishes cooked by different methods, be it broiling, steaming, stir-frying or simmering. The various dishes are served all at once and each person chooses the order in which he or she will eat them. There is no main course around which side dishes are based. Sweet dishes are included in the selection, so the meal does not end with a dessert, although fresh fruit is sometimes served.

Many dishes can be prepared in advance and served cold, thus avoiding a lot of last-minute cooking. Cooking is also done at table. One-pot meals, like *sukiyaki*, involve lengthy preparation of ingredients and then an artistic arrangement of them on platters, but the actual cooking becomes part of the enjoyment of the meal.

Each dish in a Japanese meal is thoughtfully arranged on the plate to give the most pleasing appearance. Portions are small and need not fill the entire plate. Garnishes add to the beauty of a dish, giving a contrast in color, taste and texture. Grated *daikon* or fresh gingerroot are popular, as are ornately cut vegetables, and a simple fresh flower may be used to add a seasonal touch.

Bowls, serving dishes and utensils are also chosen for their harmony with food. Individual china or black and red lacquer bowls are carefully chosen to complement the food. Small dishes are used to provide each person with an individual serving of dipping sauce or pickles.

Food is eaten with chopsticks, something that all Japanese cooks never forget when cutting up food. Soup is drunk directly from the bowl, after the pieces of vegetable, fish or meat have been eaten with chopsticks.

Meals are served with plenty of green tea (or for something a bit stronger, bottled beer or white wine goes well). In the winter months warm sake, the national alcoholic drink, can help create a lively meal.

Main ingredients

The basic foods of Japan have been and still are to a large extent grains, vegetables, seafood and soy bean products. Rice is the staple grain and it is served at every meal, including breakfast! Strict Buddhist doctrine adheres to a vegetarian diet but since World War II, as a result of American influences and changes in national attitudes, the Japanese now eat meat as well.

Rice

In Japan, rice is even more important than bread is in the West. The Japanese word for rice is *han* but the word is always given the honorable prefix *go*. Rice is therefore called *gohan*. White short-grain rice is the most popular variety with the Japanese cook and it is invariably served just plain boiled.

Compared with our way of preparing rice, the Japanese version seems to be slightly overcooked. Short-grain rice has a glutinous quality which causes the rice to stick together when cooked – this makes the rice easier to pick up with chopsticks.

The habit of eating polished white rice was started by the noble families of Japan hundreds of years ago and it is now standard practice. For this reason, most Japanese recipes are more suited to white rice than brown, although in Japan, as elsewhere, there is a growing awareness of food value and brown rice is coming back into favor.

Soy sauce, tofu and miso

Soy beans are vital to Japanese cooking but they are never eaten whole. Instead, they are processed to make three different foods which are widely used in cooking.

Soy sauce is the soy bean product most familiar to people in the West. It is made from a mixture of soy beans, wheat and salt fermented together for up to two years. The resulting mash is pressed and filtered to extract the soy sauce. There are a number of varieties, ranging in strength and color.

Unfortunately, the soy sauce widely available in the West is really flavored and colored liquid quite unlike its original inspiration. Genuinely fermented soy sauce will be more expensive but well worth the extra cost. Look out for the Japanese variety, called *shoyu*, or other authentic oriental varieties sold in Japanese markets, or specialist food stores. You can also buy most Japanese ingredients by mail order from oriental suppliers.

Soy sauce is used like salt to season dishes. It also imparts a distinctive, slightly nutty flavor to sauces and marinades.

miso is used as a soup base bean paste. The best is fermented and then aged in wooden casks for two or more years. There are, like soy sauce, a variety of misos of different strengths and colors. A good source of protein, Miso is used as a soup base and is often added to dipping sauces and marinades.

Tofu, or bean curd, is made by soaking and grinding soy beans, then extracting and curdling the liquid produced. The process is similar to that used in cheese making and, in fact, tofu has a soft delicate texture not unlike that of cottage cheese.

Like miso, tofu provides an important source of protein in the Japanese diet. White or pale cream in color, it has a slightly nutty but bland taste. When added to soups, stews and vegetable dishes, it will absorb the other flavors of the dish. It is sold fresh in Japanese markets and can be kept in cold water in the refrigerator for 2-3 days, as long as the water is changed regularly. It is also sold canned and in instant powdered form.

Noodles

Although Italy is the country most associated with pasta dishes, noodles have been eaten in Japan for centuries.

Noodles lend themselves to a wide variety of dishes and one of the pleasures of eating out in Japan is to go to one of the restaurants specializing in noodle dishes. There you can choose a bowl of steaming hot noodle soup topped with meat or vegetables, or noodles cooked with seaweed. Noodles served on their own with a simple dipping sauce and garnish are quite delicious, while, in summer, you can try noodles chilled in a salad.

There are three main types of Japanese noodle. *Udon* and *somen* are noodles made from wheat flour and are quite similar to Italian pasta. *Udon* is a flat, spaghetti-like noodle; *somen* is thin like vermicelli. *Soba* noodles are made from buckwheat flour. They are tastier and chewier than other noodles and well worth trying.

Seafood

Japan is surrounded on all sides by the sea so it is not surprising that the country is a great fish-eating nation, to such an extent that it is possible to have a fine meal that contains fish in every course.

Although they choose from an abundance of fish varieties, the Japanese enjoy much of the seafood that is familiar in the West. Mackerel, herrings and tuna are popular, as are clams, crab and shrimp. Fish and shellfish are cooked by broiling, frying, baking (in foil on top of the range), boiling and steaming.

The most famous way that the Japanese serve fish is *sashimi*, or uncooked sliced fish. Western myths about *sashimi* abound but it neither tastes nor smells fishy. It has its own subtle flavor and an exquisite texture.

When making *sashimi*, it is of paramount importance that only the freshest fish is used. Use whole fish, freshly gutted, cleaned and filleted—never use ready-filleted fish.

When buying fish look for shiny almost slimy skin and a fresh clean smell. Eyes should be bright and the gills red.

Japanese chefs spend years learning the art of thinly slicing fish for *sashimi*. However, with a very sharp knife it is not too difficult to achieve attractive raw fish dishes that will be a delight to serve.

Meat

Next to fish, chicken is the most important meat in Japanese cookery. In Japan, chicken is easily obtainable ready-boned. Chicken breast is the most favored part of the chicken because it cooks so quickly, lending itself to broiling and frying, the most popular cooking methods.

Traditionally, the Japanese do not eat large quantities of

meat. Pork or beef are served in bite-size pieces or in thin slices, combined with vegetables and rice or as part of a one-pot meal. As ovens are rare in Japan, oven roasting is virtually unknown.

Seaweed

Seaweed is the Japanese food Westerners are most disinclined to try, but in Japan seaweed is a commonplace food and its use is taken for granted. In fact, *kombu* seaweed is packaged in fancy boxes which are given as presents.

Nori, *wakame* and *kombu* are three types most widely available in the West. *Nori* seaweed is dried and pressed into sheets and used for wrapping around rice to make a sort of Japanese sandwich. *Kombu* is one of the two main ingredients in *dashi*, the basic stock. Along with *wakame*, these seaweeds add their distinctive flavors to countless Japanese dishes.

Seaweeds are sold dried in the West and can be easily reconstituted by soaking them in plenty of lukewarm water for about 10 to 15 minutes.

Vegetables

The Japanese have a high regard for their vegetables and take great care when cooking them to retain their colors, textures and flavors.

Shopping is done every day to ensure that only the freshest vegetables are used. Young, tender varieties are preferred not only for their sweet, delicate flavors but because they cook quickly yet remain crisp.

A great variety of vegetables are grown and the selection changes with each season. Leafy green vegetables are popular as are mushrooms, bamboo shoots and unusual root vegetables like burdock and lotus root. A number of unusual Japanese vegetables are available either dried or canned in the United States.

Vegetables are only lightly cooked, usually by stir-frying in oil or simmering in a minimum of water.

Little distinction is made between salads and vegetables, which are often served cold anyway. Pickled vegetables may be served where Westerners would serve salads.

Very special care is taken with cutting vegetables. Each type must be cut uniformly to make sure they cook evenly. Vegetables may be cut into a variety of shapes, ranging from simple circles or matchstick strips to more elaborate flower motifs, requiring a special skill which the Japanese are only too pleased to demonstrate.

Equipment

Most Japanese dishes can be prepared without any special equipment. A good chopping board and sharp knives are important, as are heavy-bottomed saucepans and a skillet or wok. A pestle and mortar is also useful for grinding sesame seeds and pulses and for making small amounts of purée.

For more authentic cooking, a bamboo mat, know as a *sudare*, can be used for rolling rice rolls. To make traditional one-pot meals a *sukiyaki-nabe* is used; this is a deep, cast-iron pan. Steamers, made of bamboo or metal, are useful when making steamed dishes. A rectangular omelet pan, known as *makiyaki-nabe*, is ideal for creating neatly shaped rolled omelets.

Cutting circles

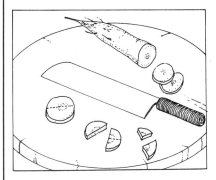

Slice vegetables such as *daikon*, into circles. Halve the circles for half moons, halve again to make quarters.

Cutting rectangles

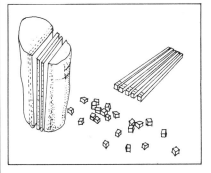

Cut 2 inch lengths of vegetables into rectangles, then cut thinly to make matchstick strips. To dice, cut the strips into small cubes.

けもの

Soups

Soup is an integral part of the Japanese meal and is always served at the same time as all the other dishes. The choice includes delicate clear soups and heartier soups, thickened with vegetables or rice – most are based on the simple Japanese stock, Dashi, which gives the distinctive, clean flavor that is so pleasing.

Japanese Stock
(Dashi)

Preparation and cooking:
10 minutes

Makes 5 cups
4 inch square piece of kombu seaweed
½ oz katsuobushi (dried bonito flakes)
5 cups water

1 Rinse the kombu and cut a ½ inch fringe along all sides of the square.

2 Pour the water into a medium-size saucepan. Add the kombu and bring the water almost to a boil over medium heat. Lift out the kombu and reserve (see below).

3 Bring the water to a boil. Stir in the katsuobushi.

4 Remove the pan from the heat and let stand for 2-3 minutes. Pour the liquid through a strainer lined with a double thickness of damp un-bleached muslin.

5 Use the stock as required – it will keep in the refrigerator for 2-3 days.

● In Japan the kombu and kat-suobushi would be used to make a second stock for bean paste soups or for cooking vegetables. The second stock is made in the same way, but with 3 cups water.

Egg drop soup (Kakitama-jiru)

Egg drop soup
(Kakitama-jiru)

Preparation and cooking:
10 minutes

Serves 4
2½ cups dashi (Japanese stock),
see page 10
¾ teaspoon salt
½ teaspoon soy sauce
1 tablespoon cornstarch, mixed
to a paste with 2 tablespoons
water
1 egg, beaten and stirred with
1 tablespoon dashi
1 teaspoon juice squeezed from
grated fresh gingerroot
For garnish
lime or lemon rind, cut in
decorative shapes

1 Pour the stock into a medium-size saucepan, cover and bring to a boil. Season with the salt and soy sauce, then stir in the cornstarch mixture over medium heat. Continue stirring until the soup is slightly thickened and smooth.

2 Lower the heat so that the soup is barely simmering. Pour in the egg mixture through a flat skimmer or a strainer, moving it in a circle over the soup. Cook for a few seconds longer to set the egg threads. Remove from the heat.

3 Add the ginger juice and pour the soup into 4 soup bowls. Garnish the soup with the decorative lime or lemon rind shapes and serve.

● To prepare the garnish, cut the lime or lemon rind into tiny V-shapes to represent pine needles. As an alternative garnish, toast a 4 inch square piece of nori seaweed on both sides for a few seconds, then crumble it over the soup.

Quick Japanese stock
(Dashi)

Preparation and cooking:
2 minutes

Makes 3 cups
*1 teaspoon dashi-no-moto
(instant dashi powder)
3 cups water*

1 Pour the water into a medium-size saucepan and bring to a boil. Add the dashi-no-moto and bring back to a boil over medium heat.

2 Boil for about 1 minute, stirring gently to blend, then remove from the heat and use as required.

• Dashi-no-moto (instant dashi powder) is available from Japanese markets and some general Oriental groceries. If difficult to obtain, chicken stock cubes may be used as a substitute, but bear in mind that the cooked dish will lose much of its authentic flavor.

Clear soup with sardine balls
(Iwashi no tsumire jiru)

Preparation and cooking:
1 hour

Serves 4-6
*5 fresh sardines, cleaned and with
the heads removed
2 tablespoons miso (bean paste)
½ inch piece of fresh gingerroot,
pared and grated
1 tablespoon flour
5 cups water
2 tablespoons soy sauce
¼ teaspoon salt
1 turnip, thinly sliced, then
quartered*
For garnish
*4 pieces of lemon rind, cut in
decorative shapes*

1 Remove the main bones from the sardines. Slit each fish through the belly cavity, then open out flat by pressing down on the back of the fish. Lift up the backbone from the head end and cut it free, removing the tail at the same time.

2 Clean the boned sardines in salted water, then pat dry on absorbent kitchen paper. Chop the fish into small pieces, then put in a blender and blend until smooth. Alternatively, pound with a pestle and mortar until smooth.

3 Stir the miso, grated ginger and flour into the sardines and beat until thoroughly combined. Using the palms of your hands, gently roll small pieces of the fish mixture into balls.

4 Pour the water into a large saucepan and bring to a boil. Drop in the fish balls and cook until they rise to the surface. Using a slotted spoon, transfer the fish balls to a plate and strain the cooking liquid into a clean pan. Stir the soy sauce and salt into the strained liquid.

5 Meanwhile, cook the turnip in boiling water for about 5 minutes until the pieces are just cooked but still crisp. Drain and reserve.

6 Reheat the strained soup liquid over medium heat and add the fish balls. Bring to a boil, then stir in the reserved turnip.

7 Ladle the soup into 4-6 bowls and garnish with the pieces of lemon rind. Serve at once.

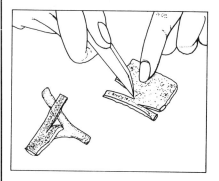

• To prepare lemon rind twists for the garnish, cut a slit into each end of a slice of rind. Trim the slice, then twist.

Clam and mushroom soup
(Hamaguri sumashi-jiru)

Preparation and cooking:
3¼ hours

Serves 4
12 littleneck clams
salt
4 cups water
8 small button mushrooms, stems removed
8 watercress sprigs
1 teaspoon soy sauce
½ cup sake
4 pieces of lemon rind

1 Cover the clams with salt water and let soak for 3 hours. Discard any that float to the surface. Drain well.

2 Pour about 4 cups water into a large saucepan and add the clams. Bring to a boil and continue to boil until the shells open. Discard any clams that do not open. Remove any foam that rises to the surface.

3 Stir in the mushroom caps, watercress and salt to taste, then cook for 1 minute. Stir in the soy sauce and the sake and bring the soup back to a boil.

4 Place 1 piece of lemon rind in each of 4 soup bowls, then divide the soup among the bowls. Serve the soup at once.

Miso soup with tofu
(Tofu no miso shiru)

Preparation and cooking:
10 minutes

Serves 4-6
5 cups dashi (Japanese stock), see page 10
4 tablespoons miso (bean paste)
1¼ cups diced tofu (bean curd)
For garnish
2 scallions, minced

1 Pour the dashi into a large saucepan and place over medium heat. Stir in the miso until it melts.

2 Raise the heat to high and add the tofu. Boil until the tofu rises to the surface of the liquid.

3 Ladle the soup into 4-6 soup bowls and garnish with the minced scallions. Serve at once.

Thick rice soup
(Zosui)

Preparation and cooking:
45 minutes

Serves 4
½ cup short-grain rice
1 sheet nori seaweed
5 cups dashi (Japanese stock), see page 10
2 inch piece of fresh gingerroot, pared and grated
salt and freshly ground black pepper
⅔ cup frozen peas, thawed
1 egg yolk, beaten

1 Rinse the rice several times until the running water is clear. Put the rice in a bowl, cover with fresh water and let to soak for 30 minutes.

2 Meanwhile, preheat the broiler to medium high. Place the nori on the broil rack and broil until it is crisp. Remove from the heat, crumble and reserve.

3 Drain the rice. Pour the dashi into a large saucepan and bring to a boil.

4 Add the rice and ginger to the pan and bring back to a boil. Reduce the heat and simmer for about 20 minutes until the rice is well cooked and starting to disintegrate.

5 Season the rice with salt and pepper to taste, then stir in the peas, crumbled nori and beaten egg yolk. Simmer for a further 10 minutes and serve at once.

Tofu soup
(Tofu no jiru)

Preparation and cooking:
1 hour

Serves 4-6
4 dried shiitake mushrooms
5 cups dashi (Japanese stock), see
page 10
3 tablespoons soy sauce
½ teaspoon salt
2 tablespoons mirin (sweet rice
wine)
2 tablespoons cornstarch, mixed
to a paste with 2 tablespoons
water
2 cups diced tofu (bean curd)
For garnish
½ inch piece of fresh gingerroot,
pared and grated

1 Soak the mushrooms in lukewarm water for 20 minutes to soften. Drain, then trim off the stems and discard. Slice the trimmed mushrooms if wished.

2 Pour the dashi into a large saucepan. Add the soy sauce, salt, mirin and soaked mushrooms, then stir in the cornstarch mixture. Bring to a boil, stirring constantly.

3 Reduce the heat to low, cover and simmer the soup for 15 minutes. Stir in the tofu and simmer for a further 5 minutes.

4 Ladle the soup into 4-6 soup bowls, dividing the tofu equally among them. Garnish each bowl with a little grated ginger and serve.

Chicken and steamed vegetables in egg (Chawan mushi) and centre, Tofu soup (Tofu no jiru)

Chicken and steamed vegetables in egg
(Chawan mushi)

Preparation and cooking:
1¼ hours

Serves 4
*1 small chicken breast, skinned,
boned and diced
soy sauce for sprinkling
2 oz firm white fish, skinned and
cut in 4 pieces
salt
½ cup thinly sliced green beans
8 shrimp, shelled
4 mushrooms, stems removed,
quartered*
Egg mixture
*4 cups dashi (Japanese stock), see
page 10
1½ teaspoon salt
1½ teaspoon soy sauce
1 teaspoon mirin (sweet rice wine)
4 eggs, plus 2 egg yolks, lightly
beaten*

1 Sprinkle the chicken pieces with soy sauce and set aside for 5 minutes. Sprinkle the fish pieces with salt and set aside.

2 Meanwhile, cook the green beans in boiling water for about 2 minutes, then drain.

3 Make the egg mixture. Mix the dashi, salt, soy sauce and mirin together. Pour the beaten eggs slowly into the mixture, stirring gently. Set aside until required.

4 Divide the chicken and fish pieces, shrimp and mushrooms among 4 small ovenproof bowls. Pour the egg mixture on top and cover, leaving the covers slightly ajar.

5 Arrange the bowls in the top of a double boiler and half fill the bottom with boiling water. (If you do not have a double boiler, use a small baking dish set in a deep roasting pan. Fill the pan with water until it comes halfway up the side of the baking dish.)

6 Steam the mixture for 25 minutes, or until the eggs have set — the surface should be yellow not brown and although the egg will be set on the outside, it should still contain some liquid inside.

7 About 5 minutes before the end of the cooking time, remove the covers from the bowls and garnish with the sliced beans. Serve hot.

● This is a soup and in Japan may also be served as a breakfast dish.

Miso soup with sautéed eggplant
(Yakinasu no misoshiru)

Preparation and cooking:
1 hour

Serves 4-6
2 eggplants, sliced
salt
½ cup vegetable oil
5 cups dashi (Japanese stock), see page 10
4 tablespoons miso (bean paste)
2 mint leaves, thinly sliced
wasabi (Japanese horseradish mustard), mixed to a paste with water

1 Put the eggplant slices into a colander and sprinkle with salt. Leave to drain for 30 minutes, then rinse under cold water and pat dry with absorbent kitchen paper.

2 Heat the oil in a skillet, add the eggplant slices and cook over medium high heat until the skin begins to burn and peel. Remove from the heat and transfer the eggplants to a chopping board. Carefully peel off the skin and chop the flesh into bite-size pieces. Divide the pieces among 4-6 soup bowls and keep hot.

3 Pour the dashi into a saucepan and bring to a boil. Stir in the miso until it melts, forming a suspension in the liquid.

4 Pour the liquid over the eggplant pieces and add some mint slices and wasabi to taste to each bowl. Serve at once.

Mussel soup
(Asarijiru)

Preparation and cooking:
2½ hours

Serves 4
20 fresh mussels
5 cups dashi (Japanese stock), see page 10
2 tablespoons mirin (sweet rice wine)
juice of 1 lemon
salt
shichimi togarashi
soy sauce

1 Thoroughly clean the mussel shells, then soak the mussels in cold water for 2 hours, changing the water several times during this period. Drain well.

2 Pour the dashi into a large saucepan, add the mussels and bring to a boil. Lower the heat and simmer gently for about 10 minutes until the shells open. Discard any mussels that do not open.

3 Add the mirin and simmer for a further 5 minutes.

4 Remove the mussels from the soup and transfer to a warmed bowl. Stir the lemon juice into the soup; season with salt, shichimi togarashi and soy sauce to taste.

5 Ladle the soup into 4 soup bowls and arrange 2 mussels, still in their shells, in each bowl. Serve at once with the remaining mussels passed around separately.

● Always buy fresh mussels on the day you are going to serve them. Select closed mussels with unbroken shells.

Pork and vegetable soup
(Butaniku to yasai shirumono)

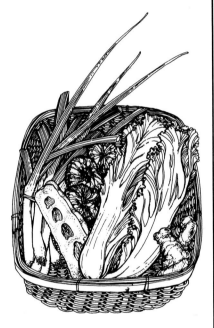

Preparation and cooking:
40 minutes

Serves 4-6
4 dried shiitake mushrooms
5 cups dashi (Japanese stock), see page 10
½ lb lean pork, thinly sliced and cut in 1 inch squares
½ cup thinly sliced canned bamboo shoots, cut in half moons
2 Chinese cabbage leaves, chopped
1 inch piece of fresh gingerroot, pared and grated
soy sauce
For garnish
2 scallions, minced

1 Soak the mushrooms in lukewarm water for 20 minutes to soften. Drain, then trim off the hard stems and discard. Slice the mushrooms.

2 Pour the dashi into a large saucepan and bring to a boil. Add the sliced pork, mushrooms, bamboo shoots, cabbage and ginger and bring back to a boil. Reduce heat and simmer for 7-8 minutes.

3 Add soy sauce to taste and ladle the soup into 4-6 soup bowls. Garnish each bowl with minced scallions and serve.

Clear soup with tofu and ginger
(Tofu to shoga no sumashijiru)

Preparation and cooking:
20 minutes

Serves 4
5 cups dashi (Japanese stock), see page 10
1 cup tofu (bean curd), cut in ½ inch cubes
2 tablespoons finely chopped fresh spinach or watercress
2 teaspoons soy sauce
2 scallions, chopped in ¼ inch lengths
1 inch piece of fresh gingerroot, pared and finely grated

1 Pour the dashi into a large saucepan and bring to a boil. Add the tofu, spinach and soy sauce. Reduce the heat and simmer gently for 10 minutes.

2 Stir in the scallions and ginger and continue to cook for a further minute.

3 Ladle the soup into 4 bowls and serve at once.

肉料理

Meat

In Japan, meat is served in small, delicate portions that delight the eye as well as the palate. Chicken and steak are particularly favored, since the lean flesh lends itself perfectly to the light cooking methods. Tasty marinades are often the key to the delicious flavors.

Sake-steamed chicken
(Tori no sakamushi)

Preparation and cooking:
1½ hours

Serves 4
4 chicken breasts, skinned, boned and cut in 1 inch slices
¾ cup sake
1 tablespoon sugar
1 teaspoon soy sauce

1 Put the chicken slices into a shallow dish and pour over the sake. Marinate at room temperature for 1 hour, basting occasionally during this time. Remove the chicken slices, reserving the marinade, and pat dry with absorbent kitchen paper.

2 Arrange the chicken slices, in one layer, in the top part of a steamer, or on an ovenproof plate. Fill the base of the steamer about two-thirds full of boiling water and fit the top part over. Cover and steam the meat for 10 minutes, then set aside.

3 Preheat the broiler to high.

4 Pour the reserved marinade into a small saucepan and stir in the sugar and soy sauce. Bring to a boil, stirring constantly, then remove from the heat.

Sake-steamed chicken (Tori no sakamushi)

5 Arrange the chicken slices on the broiler rack. Brush with the marinade sauce and broil for 3 minutes on each side, basting occasionally.

6 To serve, transfer the chicken slices to a warmed serving dish and pour over all the remaining warm marinade sauce.

Deep-fried chicken simmered in broth
(Tori no agemono-iri Shirumono)

Preparation and cooking:
45 minutes

Serves 4
vegetable oil for deep-frying
14 chicken breasts, skinned,
boned and cut in 2 inch pieces
cornstarch for dusting
4 cups dashi (Japanese stock), see
page 10
2 tablespoons soy sauce
2 tablespoons sugar
2 inch piece of fresh gingerroot
pared
3 cups Chinese cabbage, chopped
2 green peppers, seeded and
chopped
For garnish
watercress sprigs

1. Fill a heavy-bottomed saucepan with oil to a depth of 3¼ inches and heat to 350°F.

2. Dust the chicken with cornstarch and cook the pieces in batches until golden brown. Drain the chicken on absorbent kitchen paper.

3. Put the fried chicken, dashi, soy sauce, sugar, grated ginger, Chinese cabbage and green peppers in a saucepan and bring to a boil. Reduce the heat slightly and simmer for 8-10 minutes.

4. Spoon into 4 soup bowls, garnish with watercress sprigs and serve at once.

● Chicken stock may be used instead of dashi, if wished.

Chicken and mushrooms baked
(Toriniku no shichimi-yaki)

Preparation and cooking:
1 hour

Serves 4
4 dried shiitake mushrooms
4 chicken breasts
1 tablespoon vegetable oil
salt
1 lemon, cut in 4 slices
Dipping sauce
⅓ cup soy sauce
⅓ cup lemon juice
1 young leek, very thinly sliced

1. Soak the mushrooms in lukewarm water for 20 minutes. Drain them, cut away the hard stems and criss-cross the caps with shallow knife cuts.

2. Preheat the oven to 375°F.

3. Cut out 4 pieces of foil large enough to wrap each chicken breast. Brush one side of each piece of foil with oil.

4. Place 1 chicken breast on a piece of foil. Arrange a mushroom cap on top of the chicken and sprinkle the chicken and mushroom with salt. Top with a lemon slice and wrap securely in the foil. Repeat this process with the remaining chicken breasts. Bake in the oven for about 30 minutes until the chicken is cooked through.

5. Meanwhile, make the dipping sauce. Combine the soy sauce and lemon juice and divide the mixture among 4 small bowls. Top each with a little sliced leek.

6. Serve each chicken package with a small bowl of dipping sauce.

● As a general rule, the Japanese bake foil-wrapped food on top of the range. In the West, however, it is usually more convenient to use an oven – and the results are just as delicious.

Chicken sashimi with mustard dressing
(Toriwasa)

Preparation and cooking:
45 minutes

Serves 4
*2 chicken breasts, skinned and
boned
2½ cups water
2 tablespoons rice vinegar
1 cucumber, thinly sliced
salt
1 tablespoon wasabi (Japanese
horseradish mustard), mixed
to a paste with water*
For garnish
*soy sauce
1 sheet of nori seaweed*

1 Cut the boned chicken in slices about ¼ inch thick, then cut again in thin strips.

2 Pour the water into a saucepan and bring to a boil. Dip the chicken strips in the water for 30 seconds, then drain well.

3 Put the chicken in a shallow dish and sprinkle with the vinegar. Set aside.

4 Put the cucumber slices in a bowl and lightly sprinkle with salt. Set aside for about 30 minutes.

5 Meanwhile, preheat the broiler to medium high. Place the nori sheet on the rack and broil until crisp on both sides.

6 Rinse the cucumber slices under cold running water and drain. Pat dry with absorbent kitchen paper.

7 Combine the chicken strips, cucumber slices and wasabi in a serving bowl. Sprinkle with soy sauce to taste, crumble over the nori seaweed and serve.

Sauté chicken
(Niwatori no itamemono)

Preparation and cooking:
40 minutes

Serves 4
*3 tablesoons soy sauce
2 tablespoons sugar
2 tablespoons water
½ teaspoon shichimi togarashi
3 chicken breasts, skinned, boned
and cut in 2 inch pieces
3 tablespoons vegetable oil
2 scallions, minced*

1 Combine the soy sauce, sugar, water and shichimi togarashi in a small saucepan and bring to a boil. Remove from the heat.

2 Place the chicken pieces in a shallow dish and pour over the marinade. Leave to marinate for 30 minutes.

3 Heat the oil in a heavy-bottomed skillet. Remove the chicken from the marinade, and cook the chicken briskly for 6-8 minutes until browned and tender.

4 Stir in the scallions, heat through and serve.

• This dish is particularly good served on a bed of boiled rice.

Chicken rolls wrapped in nori seaweed
(Toriniku no norimaki)

Preparation and cooking:
2 hours

Serves 4
½ lb chicken breast, skinned,
boned and cooked
2 tablespoons sake
2 tablespoons soy sauce
1 sheet of nori seaweed, cut
crosswise in ½ inch wide strips
1 egg white, lightly beaten
2 tablespoons vegetable oil
For garnish
fresh gingerroot, pared and cut in
fine shreds

1 Cut the chicken breast in 2 x 1 inch pieces, ¼ inch thick.

2 Combine the sake and soy sauce in a small bowl, add the chicken pieces and marinate for about 1 hour.

3 Remove the chicken pieces from the marinade. Roll up 1 piece of chicken from the short end. Dip a strip of nori seaweed in the egg white, then tie around the roll of chicken to secure. Repeat this process for each piece of chicken.

4 Heat 1 tablespoon oil in a skillet, add half the chicken rolls and cook gently, turning once. Repeat with the remaining oil and chicken rolls.

5 Transfer to a warmed serving platter, garnish with shredded ginger and serve.

Cold ginger chicken
(Shoga-aji hiyashi toriniku)

Preparation and cooking:
2½ hours

Serves 4-6
4 chicken breasts, skinned and
boned
½ cup flour
salt and freshly ground black
pepper
2 teaspoons shichimi togarashi
⅓ cup vegetable oil
2½ cups dashi (Japanese stock),
see page 10
2 inch piece of fresh gingerroot,
pared and minced
⅓ cup mirin (sweet rice wine)
juice of 2 small oranges
1 teaspoon soy sauce
For garnish
3 × ½ inch pieces of preserved
stem ginger, cut in fine batons
4 scallions, cut in tassels

1 Cut each chicken breast into even-size strips.

2 Spread half the flour on a flat plate and season generously with salt, pepper and shichimi togarashi. Dip the chicken strips in the seasoned flour, shaking off the excess.

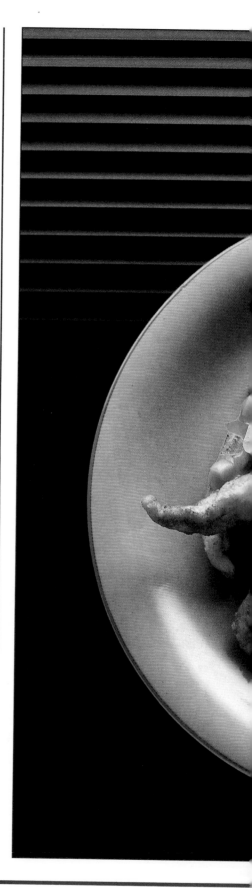

3 Heat the oil in a large skillet, add half the chicken strips and cook for 2-3 minutes on each side, or until golden brown and cooked through. Transfer them to a plate using a slotted spoon or chopsticks. Repeat with the remaining chicken strips, then cool and refrigerate.

4 Spoon ¼ cup of the oil from the skillet into a saucepan, then stir in the remaining flour and cook over a low heat for 2-3 minutes, stirring constantly.

5 Add the dashi, stirring vigorously with a wire whip to prevent lumps forming. Stir in the minced fresh ginger and the mirin. Bring the sauce to a boil and boil over a high heat until reduced to a glossy consistency and thick enough to coat the back of a wooden spoon.

6 Stir in the orange juice and soy sauce and season to taste with a little salt and black pepper. Let cool completely.

7 Arrange the cold chicken pieces on 4-6 individual dishes. Spoon over enough cold sauce to coat them lightly and garnish with batons of preserved ginger and scallion tassels. Pass the remaining sauce separately.

Cold ginger chicken (Shoga-aji hiyashi toriniku)

Barbecued chicken
(Yaki tori)

Preparation and cooking:
40 minutes

Serves 4
1 lb leeks, cleaned and cut in
½ inch lengths
3 chicken breasts, skinned, boned
and cut in bite-size pieces
Sauce
¾ cup soy sauce
¾ cup mirin (sweet
rice wine)

1 Cook the leeks in boiling water for 5 minutes, then drain well.

2 Thread the chicken and leek pieces alternately onto small skewers. Set aside.

3 Light a hibachi or charcoal grill or preheat the broiler to medium.

4 Meanwhile, make the sauce. Put the soy sauce and mirin into a small saucepan, bring to a boil, then cook for a few minutes, or until sauce begins to thicken slightly. Remove from heat and pour into a shallow dish.

5 Arrange the chicken and leek skewers on the grill rack. Grill for 3 minutes.

6 Remove the skewers from the heat and dip into the sauce mixture, to coat the food thoroughly. Return to the heat, turn the skewers and grill for a further 3 minutes. Repeat this once more, then grill until the chicken meat is cooked through.

7 Remove from the heat and dip the skewers once more in the sauce mixture before serving.

● Lamb or calf liver and green pepper pieces can also be cooked in this way.

Chicken with sesame seeds
(Goma yaki)

Preparation and cooking:
50 minutes

Serves 2-4
2 large chicken breasts, skinned,
boned and halved
⅓ cup sesame oil
2 tablespoons sesame seeds,
roasted
Marinade
⅓ cup sake
2 teaspoons soy sauce
¼ teaspoon shichimi togarishi

1 Prepare the marinade. Combine all the marinade ingredients in a medium-size shallow dish, beating until thoroughly blended.

2 Add the chicken pieces and baste well. Leave to marinate at room temperature for 20 minutes, turning and basting the chicken occasionally. Remove from the marinade and pat dry with absorbent kitchen paper. Discard the marinade.

3 Heat the oil in a large skillet, add chicken pieces and cook for 5 minutes on each side. Sprinkle over half the sesame seeds and stir and turn until the chicken is coated. Reduce the heat to low and cook the chicken for a further 6-8 minutes, or until the pieces are cooked through and tender.

4 Transfer the mixture to a warmed serving dish and sprinkle over the remaining sesame seeds before serving.

Chicken casserole
(Iri dori)

Preparation and cooking:
1 hour

Serves 4
4 dried shiitake mushrooms
¼ cup vegetable oil
2 small chicken breasts, skinned,
boned and cut in bite-size pieces
2 large carrots, diced
1 cup chopped drained canned
bamboo shoots
¾ cup dashi (Japanese stock), see
page 10
¼ cup mirin (sweet rice wine)
¼ cup sugar
¼ cup soy sauce
3 tablespoons frozen peas

1 Soak the dried shiitake mushrooms in lukewarm water for 20 minutes to soften. Drain, then remove stems and quarter the mushrooms.

2 Heat the oil in a large, deep skillet, add the chicken pieces, mushrooms, carrots and bamboo shoots and cook for 2 minutes, stirring occasionally.

3 Add the dashi, mirin and sugar and cook for a further 10 minutes, stirring occasionally. Reduce the heat to low and stir in the soy sauce. Simmer the mixture until about three-fourths of the liquid has evaporated. Stir in the peas, cook for 3 minutes, then remove the pan from the heat.

4 Transfer the mixture to a warmed serving dish and serve at once.

• Any vegetable can be used in this dish – try sliced onions, cauliflower flowerets and brussels sprouts.

Chicken meatballs and miso
(Torigan no miso-ni)

Preparation and cooking:
30 minutes

Serves 4
2 cups ground chicken
1 onion, minced
1 canned bamboo shoot, finely
diced
2 teaspoons sugar
1 tablespoon miso (bean paste)
1 egg, beaten
2 tablespoons flour
vegetable oil for deep-frying
For garnish
1 tablespoon wasabi (Japanese
horseradish mustard), mixed to
a paste with water

1 Combine the chicken, onion, bamboo shoot, sugar, miso, egg and flour in a large bowl. Using the palms of your hands, gently shape the mixture into small balls about 1 inch in diameter.

2 Fill a heavy-bottomed saucepan with oil to a depth of 3¼ inches and heat to 350°F. Carefully lower a few meatballs into the hot oil and cook until golden brown.

3 Using a slotted spoon or chopsticks, remove the meatballs from the pan and drain on absorbent kitchen paper. Keep hot while cooking the remaining meatballs in the same way.

4 Arrange the meatballs in 4 small bowls and garnish each portion with wasabi. Serve at once.

Chicken teriyaki 1

**Preparation and cooking:
45 minutes**

Serves 4
½ cup sake
¼ cup soy sauce
*½ cup dashi (Japanese stock), see
page 10*
2 teaspoons sugar
2 teaspoons cornstarch
*4 chicken breasts, skinned and
boned*
For garnish
2 celery stalks, sliced lengthwise
8 scallions, trimmed

 Warm the sake in a small saucepan. Remove from the heat and carefully ignite, allowing the sake to burn until the flames die down. Stir in the soy sauce and dashi.

2 Put 3 tablespoons of the sake mixture in a small bowl and mix in the sugar and cornstarch. Set aside. Pour the remaining sauce into a shallow dish.

3 Preheat the broiler to medium high.

4 Dip the chicken pieces into the sauce in the shallow dish to coat thoroughly, then arrange them on the broiler rack. Broil for about 6 minutes, or until one side is golden brown.

5 Remove the chicken from heat, coat thoroughly in the sauce again and return to the rack, browned side down. Broil the other side for 6 minutes, or until golden brown. Remove from the heat again and dip into the sauce, then return to the broil rack.

Chicken teriyaki 1

6 Brush generously with the cornstarch mixture and broil for a final 6 minutes, turning the chicken occasionally, or until the meat is cooked through.

7 Arrange the chicken pieces on a warmed serving plate and garnish with the celery and scallions. Serve at once.

● The essence of Japanese cooking is well illustrated in this dish – the simplicity of presentation and the importance attached to the appearance of the dish. Cut the meat in thin strips if you wish to eat with chopsticks.

Chicken teriyaki 2

Preparation and cooking:
2¾ hours

Serves 6
2 tablespoons clear honey
6 small chicken breasts, skinned and boned
Marinade
½ cup soy sauce
salt and freshly ground black pepper
1½ inch piece of fresh gingerroot, pared and chopped
1 garlic clove, crushed
½ cup sake

1 Combine all the marinade ingredients in a shallow dish and set aside.

2 Heat the honey in a small saucepan until it melts slightly. Off heat, brush the honey generously over the chicken breasts.

3 Arrange the chicken in the marinade and leave to marinate at room temperature for 2 hours, turning and basting occasionally.

4 Preheat the oven to 350°F.

5 Line a deep-sided baking pan with foil and arrange the chicken breasts on the foil. Pour the marinade over the chicken. Bake in the oven, basting frequently, for 30-35 minutes, or until the chicken is cooked through and tender.

6 Remove from the oven and, using a slotted spoon, transfer the chicken to a warmed serving dish. Pour the cooking juices into a warmed serving bowl and serve with the chicken.

Beef with sesame seeds and vegetables
(Goma to yasai-tsuki gyu)

Preparation and cooking:
30 minutes

Serves 4
*¾ lb lean beef, cut in ¼ inch
thick slices
2 tablespoons sake
salt
3 tablespoons sesame oil
2 tablespoons sesame seeds
2 green peppers, seeded and
sliced
2 cups beansprouts, washed and
drained
soy sauce*
For garnish
finely shredded stem lettuce

1 Score the surface of each slice of beef very lightly with a sharp knife. Sprinkle with the sake and a little salt. Set aside for 15-20 minutes.

2 Heat 2 tablespoons oil in a skillet, add the beef and sauté over medium heat until tender and browned on both sides. Remove the beef from the pan and set aside.

3 Add the remaining oil to the pan, add the sesame seeds and cook over brisk heat, stirring, until just browned. Add the sliced green pepper and continue to cook for about a minute.

4 Add the beansprouts and cook until wilted. Return the beef to the pan and heat through. Season to taste with soy sauce.

5 Divide the beef mixture among 4 small bowls and garnish with finely shredded stem lettuce. Serve the beef at once.

Deep-fried beef with spiced daikon
(Momiji-oroshi-tsuki gyu no agemono)

Preparation and cooking:
at least 2¾ hours

Serves 4
*1 daikon (Japanese white radish),
about 8 inches long
and 3 inches wide
2 red chilies, seeded and
cut in half
1 lb lean beef, cut in ¼ inch thick
slices
2 tablespoons sake
2 tablespoons soy sauce
cornstarch for dusting
vegetable oil for deep-frying*
For garnish
*½ lb green beans, sliced
diagonally in 2 inch lengths and
blanched in salted water*

1 Cut the daikon in half. Make 2 small holes, the diameter of a pencil, in each end of the 2 halves of daikon and push half a chili into each hole. Leave in the refrigerator for 2-3 hours.

2 Cut the beef slices in strips measuring 1 x 3 inches. Combine the sake and soy sauce in a shallow dish, add the beef strips and marinate for 2 hours.

3 Remove the beef from the marinade and pat dry with absorbent kitchen paper. Dust the strips in cornstarch.

4 Remove the chilies from the daikon and finely grate the daikon. Return the daikon to the refrigerator.

5 Fill a heavy-bottomed saucepan with oil to a depth of 3¼ inches and heat to 350°F. Cook a batch of beef strips until golden brown. Drain on absorbent kitchen paper and keep warm while cooking the remaining strips.

6 Divide the beef among 4 bowls, arrange the grated daikon on top of each portion. Garnish with the green beans and serve at once.

Sesame-marinated steaks
(Gyuniku no amiyaki)

Preparation and cooking:
1 hour

Serves 4
4 x ½ lb rump steaks
Marinade
1½ tablespoons sesame seeds
1 garlic clove, crushed
1½ tablespoons soy sauce
1 tablespoon sake
1 teaspoon sugar
Dipping sauce
2 scallions, minced
1½ in piece of fresh gingerroot,
pared and grated
½ teaspoon shichimi togarashi
⅔ cup soy sauce
2 tablespoons dashi (Japanese
stock), see page 10

1 Prepare the marinade. Sauté the sesame seeds gently in a small skillet until they begin to "pop". Transfer to a mortar and crush with a pestle to release the oil.

2 Put the crushed seeds into a shallow dish and mix thoroughly with the remaining marinade ingredients. Add the steaks to the dish and baste well. Leave to marinate at room temperature for 30 minutes, turning the steaks and basting them occasionally.

3 Meanwhile, prepare the dipping sauce by mixing all the ingredients together. Pour the sauce into individual dipping bowls and set aside.

4 Preheat the broiler to medium high.

5 Remove the steaks from the marinade and arrange on the broiler rack. Broil for 2 minutes on each side, then reduce the heat to medium and broil for a further 2 minutes on each side for rare steaks; double the cooking time for medium steaks.

6 Remove the steaks from the heat, transfer to a chopping board and carefully cut in strips. Arrange the strips on individual serving plates. Serve at once with the dipping sauce.

Beef meatballs
(Gyuhikiniku no dango)

Preparation and cooking:
40 minutes

Serves 4-6
1¼ lb ground beef
4 scallions, minced
1½ inch piece of fresh gingerroot,
pared and grated
3 tablespoons flour
1 tablespoon soy sauce
3 eggs, lightly beaten
vegetable oil for deep-frying

1 Combine the beef, scallions, ginger, flour, soy sauce and eggs in a large bowl. Using the palms of your hands, gently shape the mixture in small balls about 1 inch in diameter.

2 Fill a heavy-based saucepan with oil to a depth of 3¼ inches and heat to 350°F. Carefully lower the meatballs, a few at a time, into the hot oil and cook until they are golden brown.

3 Using a slotted spoon or chopsticks, remove the meatballs from the pan and drain on absorbent kitchen paper. Keep hot while cooking the remaining meatballs in the same way.

4 To serve, thread on to 4-6 short skewers, putting 3-4 meatballs on each.

Beef teriyaki 1

Preparation and cooking:
1¼ hours

Serves 4
1 lb fillet steak
3 tablespoons vegetable oil
Marinade
¼ cup sake
2 tablespoons soy sauce
1 garlic clove, crushed
¼ cup dashi (Japanese stock), see page 10
For garnish
1 tablespoon vegetable oil
2 teaspoons lemon juice
1 teaspoon soy sauce
½ teaspoon sugar
shichimi togarashi
1 sweet red pepper, seeded and diced
finely chopped chives

1 Cut the fillet in 3 x 1 inch lengths.

2 Make the marinade. Combine all the marinade ingredients in a large shallow bowl. Arrange the steak in the mixture and leave to marinate at room temperature for 1 hour, turning th steak and basting occasionallly.

3 Meanwhile, prepare the garnish. Combine the oil lemon juice, soy sauce, sugar and schichimi togarashi to taste in a small bowl. Add the sweet red pepper, toss to coat well and set aside.

4 Remove the steak lengths, reserving the marinade, then pat dry on absorbent kitchen paper.

5 Heat the oil in a large skillet, add steaks and sauté for 1 minute on each side. Pour off all but a thin film of fat from the pan and add the marinade. Cook the steak for a further 3 minutes on each side, basting occasionally with the pan juices. These times will give rare steak; double the cooking time for medium.

6 Transfer the steak lengths to warmed serving plates and pour a little of the pan juices over the meat, if wished. Arrange a small portion of the sweet red pepper garnish beside each portion of steak. Sprinkle the steak and pepper garnish with chopped chives and serve at once.

Beef teriyaki 1

Beef teriyaki 2

Preparation and cooking:
2¼ hours

Serves 6
1½ lb fillet steak, cut in ¼ inch
slices
Marinade
1 inch piece of fresh gingerroot,
pared and chopped
2 garlic cloves, crushed
4 scallions, minced
2 tablespoons light brown sugar
1 cup soy sauce
½ cup sake
salt and freshly ground black
pepper

1 Combine all the marinade
ingredients in a large shallow dish. Put the steak slices in
the marinade and leave to
marinate at room temperature
for about 2 hours, basting
occasionally.

2 Preheat the broiler to
high.

3 Remove the steak slices
from the marinade and
arrange on the broiler rack.
Brush generously with the
marinade mixture and broil for
2 minutes. Remove the steak
slices from the heat, turn over
and brush with the marinade,
then broil for a further 2 minutes for rare steak; double the
cooking time for medium
steak.

4 Transfer the steak slices to
warmed serving dishes
and serve at once, or cut in
thin strips before serving.

Beef kabobs with green pepper
(Gyuniku no kushiyaki)

Preparation and cooking:
1½ hours

Serves 4
1 lb rump steak, cut in bite-size
cubes
1 large green pepper, seeded and
cut in pieces about the same size
as the meat cubes
1 large sweet red pepper, seeded
and cut in pieces about the same
size as the meat cubes
½ cup flour
2 eggs, beaten
¾ cup dried bread crumbs
vegetable oil for deep-frying
Marinade
⅓ cup soy sauce
3 tablespoons mirin (sweet rice
wine)
2 scallions, chopped
1 teaspoon sugar
½ teaspon shichimi togarishi

1 Make the marinade. Put
all the ingredients in a
large shallow dish and mix
until they are thoroughly
blended.

2 Thread the steak cubes
and pepper pieces onto
the skewers, then arrange
them carefully in the marinade
mixture. Leave to marinate at
room temperature for at least
1 hour, turning the skewers
occasionally so that all sides of
the meat and pepper pieces
are coated in the marinade.

3 Remove the meat and
pepper skewers, then discard the marinade. Pat the
cubes dry with absorbent
kitchen paper. Put the flour,
beaten eggs and bread crumbs
in separate dishes. Dip the
skewers lightly in the flour,
shaking off any excess. Dip
into the beaten eggs, then coat
evenly with the bread crumbs,
shaking off any excess.

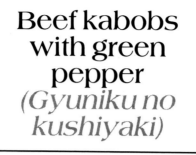

4 Fill a large, deep skillet about one-third full with vegetable oil and heat until very hot. Carefully lower the skewers, a few at a time, into the oil and fry the beef and peppers until they are crisp and golden brown. Remove from the oil and drain on absorbent kitchen paper.

5 Transfer the skewers to a warmed serving plate and serve at once.

● This dish is a sort of Japanese shaslik and the "extra" fillings can be varied according to taste. The combination here is particularly colorful, but you could substitute whole pearl onions, tomatoes and mushrooms if wished.

Deep-fried pork kabobs
(Buta kushikatsu)

Preparation and cooking: 40 minutes

Serves 4
1 lb lean pork, cut in ½ inch cubes
1 small eggplant, cut in 1 inch cubes, salted, and rinsed
2 green peppers, seeded and cut in 1 inch squares
1 cup small button mushrooms
1 onion, cut into chunks
salt and freshly ground black pepper
½ cup flour
2 eggs, beaten
1½ cups soft white bread crumbs
vegetable oil for deep-frying
For garnish
lemon wedges

1 Thread the lean pork and eggplant cubes, green pepper squares, mushrooms and onions onto skewers in a colorful arrangement. Season each skewer with salt and black pepper to taste.

2 Put the flour, beaten eggs and bread crumbs in separate dishes. Dip the skewers lightly in flour, shaking off any excess. Dip into the beaten egg, then coat thoroughly with the bread crumbs, shaking off any excess.

3 Fill a large, deep skillet about one-third full with vegetable oil and heat until very hot. Carefully lower a few of the skewers into the oil and cook for 5 minutes until golden brown. Drain on absorbent kitchen paper and keep warm while cooking the remaining kabobs.

4 Transfer to a warmed serving platter, garnish with lemon wedges and serve at once.

Kidneys in sauce (Jinzo no nikomi)

Kidneys in sauce
(Jinzo no nikomi)

Preparation and cooking:
1 hour

Serves 4
1/4 cup soy sauce
3 tablespoons sake
2 tablespoons honey
1 1/4 cups dashi (Japanese stock),
see page 10
1 garlic clove, crushed
8 lamb kidneys, slit in half
lengthwise, core removed
1/4 cup flour, for coating
salt and freshly ground black
pepper
3 tablespoons vegetable oil
1 tablespoon cornstarch
For garnish
scallions, chopped or cut in
tassels

1 In a bowl, mix together the soy sauce, sake, honey, dashi and garlic. Add the kidneys, making sure they are well coated with the mixture. Cover the bowl and leave to marinate at room temperature for 30 minutes.

2 Remove the kidneys from the bowl with a slotted spoon, reserving the marinade. Pat the kidneys dry with absorbent kitchen paper. Put the flour on a plate and season with salt and pepper. Dip the kidneys in the seasoned flour to coat thoroughly.

3 Heat the oil in a large skillet, add the kidneys and sauté over medium heat for about 5 minutes until browned on all sides and just cooked through.

4 Meanwhile, mix the cornstarch to a smooth paste with a little of the reserved marinade in a saucepan. Stir in the remaining marinade, bring to a boil, stirring, then lower the heat and simmer gently until the sauce is thick.

5 Add the cooked kidneys to the sauce and turn to coat. Taste and adjust seasoning, then transfer to a warmed serving dish and garnish with scallions. Serve at once.

Pork with sake
(Buta no kakuni)

Preparation and cooking:
3 1/2-4 hours

Serves 4
1 1/4 lb lean pork, cut in
4 pieces
1 1/2 inch piece of fresh gingerroot,
pared and sliced
2 garlic cloves, sliced
2 cups sake
1/4 cup sugar
1/3 cup soy sauce
1/2 teaspoon salt
1 tablespoon wasabi (Japanese
horse-radish mustard), mixed to a
paste with water

1 Put the pork in a medium-size saucepan and add just enough water to cover. Stir in the ginger and the sliced garlic.

2 Bring to a boil, reduce the heat to low and simmer for 1 hour. Off heat, cool, then skim any fat from the surface of the liquid.

3 Add the sake and sugar and continue to simmer for about 1 1/2 hours, or until the meat is so tender that it is almost coming apart. Stir in the soy sauce and salt and remove the pan from the heat.

4 To serve, divide the pork among 4 deep serving plates and pour over the cooking liquid. Add a dash of wasabi to each piece of meat and serve at once.

Japanese pork scallops (Tonkatsu)

Preparation and cooking:
2½ hours

Serves 6
6 large slices of pork tenderloin, beaten thin
2 eggs, beaten
2 tablespoons minced scallions
2 cups fresh white bread crumbs
⅓ cup vegetable oil
Marinade
⅓ cup soy sauce
¼ cup mirin (sweet rice wine)
2 garlic cloves, crushed
1 teaspoon shichimi togarishi
For garnish
shichimi togarishi

1 Make the marinade. Combine the soy sauce, mirin, garlic and shichimi togarishi together, beating until they are thoroughly blended.

2 Arrange the pork scallops in the marinade and leave to marinate at room temperature for 20 minutes, turning and basting the pork occasionally. Remove from the marinade and pat dry with absorbent kitchen paper. Discard the marinade.

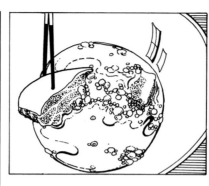

3 Mix the eggs and scallion together in a shallow bowl. Put the bread crumbs in another bowl. Dip the pork, first in the egg, then in the bread crumbs, shaking off any excess. Arrange the coated pork pieces on a plate and place in the refrigerator for 2 hours to chill.

4 Heat the oil in a large skillet, add the pork and fry for 3-4 minutes on each side, or until they are golden brown and crisp. Remove from the heat and drain on absorbent kitchen paper.

5 Cut the pork scallops crosswise in thin strips, then carefully reassemble into the scallop shape. Serve at once, garnished with a sprinkling of shichimi togarishi to taste.

● The pork scallops are divided in thin strips before serving to enable chopstick users to pick up the meat easily. If you plan to eat with a knife and fork, this step can be omitted.

Boiled pork (Yudebutaniku no nikomi)

Preparation and cooking:
1½ hours

Serves 4
1½ lb boneless pork loin
1½ inch piece of fresh gingerroot, pared and thinly sliced
2 tablespoons sake
¼ cup soy sauce
4 teaspoons sugar
2 inch piece of scallion, white part only, minced

1 Cut the piece of pork in half so that it fits into a medium-size saucepan comfortably in one layer. Pour in just enough water to barely cover. Bring to the simmering point, lower the heat and simmer, uncovered, for 1 hour or until the pork is tender and most of the water has evaporated. Drain and discard the stock. Rinse out the saucepan.

2 Cool the pork slightly and cut it in 1 inch cubes. Return the cubes to the saucepan.

3 Add the ginger, sake, half the soy sauce and 1 tablespoon sugar. Add enough water barely to cover. Simmer, covered, over medium heat for 10 minutes.

4 Add the rest of the soy sauce and sugar and simmer, uncovered, until the liquid has evaporated.

5 Divide the pork among 4 small bowls and sprinkle with minced scallion. Serve at once.

Pork with tofu and cucumber
(Tofu to kyuri-iri butaniku)

Preparation and cooking:
25 minutes

Serves 4
2 tablespoons vegetable oil
2 garlic cloves, minced
1 lb lean pork, cut in
¾ inch cubes
1 cup sliced canned bamboo
shoots
1 cup sliced mushrooms
3 tablespoons soy sauce, mixed
with
3 tablespoons water
1 cup tofu (bean curd), cut in
1 inch cubes
½ small cucumber, sliced and cut
in half moons
For garnish
2 scallions, cut into tassels

1 Heat the oil in a heavy-bottomed saucepan, add the garlic and pork cubes and cook over brisk heat, stirring, until the pork is browned all over.

2 Reduce the heat and stir in the bamboo shoots and mushrooms. Cook for a further 1 minute, stirring. Add the soy sauce mixture, cover the pan and simmer for 5 minutes.

3 Stir in the tofu cubes and cucumber half moons and cook, stirring, until heated through.

4 Transfer to individual serving plates and garnish with scallion tassels. Serve at once.

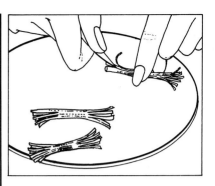

● To make scallion tassels for the garnish, trim the scallions of most of the green tops and remove the thin skin and bulb end. With a sharp knife, make several slits close together at either end of the trimmed scallions.

Place the onions in a bowl of ice water for 1 hour. The tops will curl back to make "tassels". Drain and use them as required.

Seafood

Seafood is probably the most important ingredient in Japanese cookery. The raw fish delicacy, Sashimi, epitomizes the Japanese flair for presentation, but there are also many cooked dishes which will appeal to all tastes. Cooking methods range from frying to steaming – Tempura, a tempting selection of deep-fried seafood in batter, is just one fine example.

Fish barbecued with salt
(Sakana shioyaki)

Preparation and cooking:
50 minutes

Serves 4
4 herring, cleaned and gutted
3 tablespoons salt

1 Pat the fish dry and sprinkle with salt. Let stand at room temperature for at least 30 minutes.

2 Light a hibachi or charcoal grill or preheat the broiler to medium.

3 Wipe any excess liquid from the fish and sprinkle with a little more salt, rubbing it well into the tail to prevent burning.

4 Arrange the fish on the grill rack and grill for 15-20 minutes, turning occasionally, until the fish flakes easily. Serve at once.

● This simple way of preparing fish is very popular in Japan and preserves all the natural flavor of the fish.

Barbecued mackerel fillets (Saba no shioyaki)

Barbecued mackerel fillets
(Saba no shioyaki)

Preparation and cooking:
45 minutes

Serves 4
*1 mackerel, cleaned and filleted
salt
²/₃ cup grated daikon (Japanese
white radish)
4 lemon slices*

1 Light a hibachi or charcoal grill or preheat the broiler to medium. Cut the fillets in half crosswise and sprinkle with salt. Leave for 30 minutes.

2 Rinse in cold water and pat dry with absorbent kitchen paper. Cut a shallow cross in the skin of each piece, taking care not to cut into the flesh.

3 Arrange the fish on the grill rack. Grill for 2 minutes each side, turning once.

4 Arrange the grilled fish on 4 small plates, skin side up. Lightly squeeze out moisture from the daikon. Place a mound on each lemon slice and arrange on each plate.

Fish teriyaki

Preparation and cooking:
40 minutes

Serves 4
*4 mackerel or herring, cleaned
and gutted
2 tablespoons fresh lemon juice
2 tablespoons soy sauce
2 tablespoons vegetable oil*
For garnish
*2-3 tablespoons poppy seeds
thinly pared lemon rind*

1 Preheat the broiler to medium.

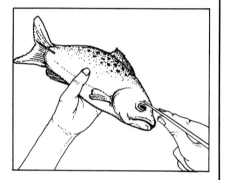

2 Skewer the fish: insert a skewer near the eye of the fish, then thread it along the length of the fish by bending it up toward the top of the fins and then down again to the center. Do not pierce the skin on the other side of the fish. Bring the skewer out at the tail end on an upward movement.

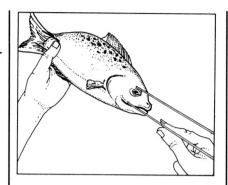

3 Insert a second skewer near the mouth and repeat the process, bringing this skewer out below the tail.

4 Put the lemon juice in a small bowl with the soy sauce and vegetable oil. Mix well together. Brush the fish with the mixture.

5 Arrange the fish on the broil rack and broil for about 12 minutes, turning occasionally and brushing with the lemon mixture. The fish is cooked when the flesh flakes easily.

6 Transfer to a warmed serving dish, garnish with poppy seeds and lemon rind and serve.

● The method used for skewering the fish is termed as "stitching". Once "stitched", the fish retains its shape during cooking.

Barbecued sardines
(Iwashi no su-jyoyu zuke)

Preparation and cooking:
2¼ hours

Serves 4
*⅔ cup soy sauce
¼ cup rice vinegar
2 tablespoons lemon juice
1 inch piece of fresh gingerroot,
pared and chopped
2 garlic cloves, crushed
1 lb fresh sardines, cleaned and
gutted
2 tablespoons vegetable oil*

1 Combine the soy sauce, vinegar, lemon juice, ginger and garlic in a bowl. Arrange the sardines in a large shallow dish and pour over the soy sauce mixture, basting to coat the fish thoroughly. Leave to marinate at room temperature for 2 hours, basting the fish occasionally.

2 Remove the sardines from the marinade and dry them on absorbent kitchen paper. Discard the marinade.

3 Light a hibachi or charcoal grill or preheat the broiler to medium high.

4 Arrange the sardines on the grill rack and brush with half the oil. Grill for 4 minutes, then turn the fish over and brush with the remaining oil. Grill for 3 minutes, or until the flesh flakes easily.

5 Remove from the heat and serve at once.

Small fish cakes
(Kamaboko)

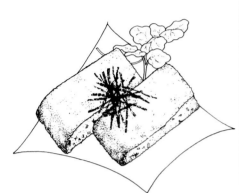

Preparation and cooking:
30 minutes

Serves 4-6
*1 lb white fish fillets, skinned and chopped
3 tablespoons flour
2 egg whites, beaten until frothy
1 tablespoon mirin (sweet rice wine)
1 teaspoon sugar
½ cup cornstarch
⅓ cup vegetable oil*

1 Put the fish pieces into a blender or food processor and work to a fairly smooth purée. Transfer the purée to a mixing bowl and stir in the flour, egg whites, mirin and sugar. Beat briskly until the fish mixture is thoroughly blended.

2 Take about 2 tablespoons of the mixture and shape it into a small cake or patty shape. Dust lightly with cornstarch and set aside. Repeat until all the mixture is used up.

3 Heat the oil in a large skillet, add the fish cakes (in batches, if necessary) and cook gently for 5 minutes on each side, or until they are golden brown and crisp, and cooked through.

4 Remove from the pan with a slotted spoon or chop sticks and drain on absorbent kitchen paper.

• Kamaboko are very popular in Japan as an hors d'ouevre, but they can also form part of some one-pot meals. Almost any type of white fish fillet can be used. The fish cakes can be steamed instead of fried if preferred. This gives them a more delicate flavor.

Fish cooked in
soy sauce
(Nizakana)

Preparation and cooking:
30 minutes

Serves 4
*4 herring, cleaned and gutted
1½ inch piece of fresh gingerroot, pared and sliced*
Sauce
*1 cup dashi (Japanese stock), see page 10
1 cup soy sauce
1 cup sake
1 tablespoon sugar*

1 Put the fish on a chopping board and make 2 or 3 cuts through the belly of each one to allow the sauce to be absorbed while cooking. Set aside.

2 Put the dashi, soy sauce, sake and sugar in a saucepan large enough to hold the fish. Bring to a boil.

3 Arrange the fish in the bottom of the pan and sprinkle the ginger slices over the top. Return the dashi mixture to a boil, reduce the heat to low and simmer for 5 minutes. Reduce the heat to very low and continue to simmer for a further 15 minutes.

4 Transfer the fish to a warmed deep serving dish and pour over some of the cooking liquid. Serve at once.

• Other types of fish, such as mackerel, butterfish, pompano and sardine, can be used instead of herring in this dish.

Deep-fried roes
(Kazuno kono agemono)

**Preparation and cooking:
1½ hours**

Serves 4
*12 large soft herring roes
salt
vegetable oil for deep-frying*
Batter
*1 cup flour
pinch of salt
1 tablespoon olive oil
¾ cup lukewarm water
1 large egg white*
For garnish
*watercress sprigs
1 lemon, quartered*

Deep-fried roes (Kazuno Kono agemono)

1 Blanch the roes. Bring a large saucepan of salted water to a boil, add the roes, bring back to the boil and cook for 2 minutes. Drain and pat dry them.

2 Make the batter. Sift the flour and salt into a bowl, stir in the oil and beat in the lukewarm water. Cover and set aside for 1 hour.

3 Fill a small, heavy-bottomed saucepan with oil to a depth of 3¼ inches and heat to 400°F. Beat the egg white until stiff and lightly fold into the batter.

4 Dip the roes into the batter, shake off any excess and cook them, a few at a time, in the hot oil. Remove the roes, drain on absorbent kitchen paper and keep warm.

5 Arrange on a serving dish, garnish with the watercress and lemon and serve.

Barbecued mackerel with miso
(Saba no misozuke)

Preparation and cooking: Marinating, then 20 minutes

Serves 4
4 mackerel, cleaned, gutted and cut into 2 inch pieces
Marinade
¼ lb miso (bean paste)
¼ cup sugar
2 tablespoons sake
2 tablespoons mirin (sweet rice wine)

1 Make the marinade. Combine all the ingredients in a large, shallow bowl, beating until they are thoroughly blended. Arrange the fish pieces in the marinade, basting to coat completely. Cover the dish and chill in the refrigerator for at least 1 day, turning the fish pieces occasionally.

2 Remove the fish pieces from the marinade and pat dry with absorbent kitchen paper. Discard the marinade.

3 Light a hibachi or charcoal grill or preheat the broiler to medium. Arrange the fish pieces on the broiler rack and broil for 5 minutes. Turn the fish over and broil for 5-8 minutes more, or until the flesh flakes easily.

4 Transfer the fish pieces to a warmed serving dish and serve at once.

● Any similar rather oily fish could be substituted for the mackerel — herring, fresh large sardines, or even red mullet or kingfish.

Mackerel simmered with miso
(Sakana miso-yaki)

Preparation and cooking:
1½ hours

Serves 4
4 tablespoons miso (bean paste)
½ cup water
1 tablespoon sugar
2 inch piece of fresh gingerroot,
pared and grated
4 mackerel, cleaned, gutted and
heads removed
juice of 1 lemon
For garnish
¼ lb green beans, blanched in
salted water

1 Cream the miso with a little of the water in a bowl, then beat in the sugar, ginger and remaining water.

2 Place the fish in a large shallow dish and pour over the miso sauce. Leave to marinate for 1 hour.

3 Transfer the fish and marinade to a skillet and bring to a boil. Reduce the heat and simmer gently for 10 minutes until the fish is tender but still firm.

4 Sprinkle the fish with lemon juice and transfer to a warmed serving dish. Garnish with green beans and serve at once.

● For mackerel in sour miso, replace the water with a mild vinegar. Herring and sardines are also delicious cooked in this way.

Fish in wine sauce
(Sakana no wain sosu nikomi)

Preparation and cooking:
40 minutes

Serves 4
4 large herring, cleaned, gutted
and filleted
¼ cup sake
¼ cup mirin (sweet rice wine)
½ cup soy sauce
2 tablespoons sugar
For garnish
1 teaspoon freshly ground black
pepper
1 tablespoon chopped fresh
parsley
1 teaspoon chopped chives

1 Put the fish on a chopping board and cut each one in two lengthwise. Make 3 cuts on the skin side of each fish, taking care not to cut through the flesh completely. Set aside until required.

2 Put the sake and mirin into a small saucepan and bring to a boil. Off heat, ignite carefully. Leave until the flames have died down, then stir in the soy sauce and sugar. Pour the mixture into a shallow mixing bowl.

3 Preheat the broiler to medium.

4 Dip the herring into the sauce mixture, then arrange them on the broiler rack. Broil for 5 minutes. Remove the fish from the heat and dip into the sauce again. Return to the heat, turning the fish the other way up, and cook for a further 5 minutes.

5 Transfer the fish to a warmed serving dish and garnish with the pepper, parsley and chives. Pour the basting liquid into a warmed serving bowl and serve with the fish.

Baked fish with vegetables
(Yakizakana)

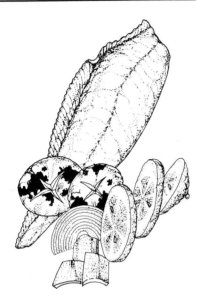

Preparation and cooking:
50 minutes

Serves 4
*4 dried shiitake mushrooms or
4 large mushrooms
1 lb white fish fillets
vegetable oil for greasing
1 onion, sliced
2 green peppers, seeded and
quartered
4 teaspoons sake or white wine
salt and freshly ground black
pepper
1 lemon, sliced
soy sauce*

1 Soak the dried shiitake mushrooms (if using) in lukewarm water for 20 minutes to soften. Drain. Trim the stems of the mushrooms. Using a sharp knife, cut a criss-cross design on the caps.

2 Cut the fish in 4 pieces and cut 8 pieces of foil, measuring 6 x 10 inches.

3 Preheat the oven to 425°F.

4 Lightly grease 4 pieces of foil and, on each piece, arrange the following: onion slices, fish, green pepper and a mushroom. Season with sake and salt and pepper to taste, then top with a slice of lemon and wrap tightly in foil. Wrap each foil package in another piece of foil. Bake in the oven for 15-20 minutes.

5 Remove the foil parcels from the oven, open the foil and sprinkle each portion with soy sauce to taste. Serve at once, straight from the foil.

Cod's roes and vegetables in soy sauce
(Tarako to yasai no niawase)

Preparation and cooking:
30 minutes

Serves 4-6
*2 oz canned shirataki noodles
3 tablespoons vegetable oil
1 large carrot, but in matchstick
strips
1 tablespoon sake
2 fresh cod's roes, skinned
1 cup dashi (Japanese stock), see
page 10
2 tablespoons soy sauce
1 tablespoon mirin
1 leek, finely chopped*

1 Soak the shirataki noodles in hot water for 3 minutes. Drain and cut in matchstick strips.

2 Heat the oil in a deep skillet, add the carrot, shirataki noodles and sake. Cook, stirring occasionally, for 5 minutes.

3 Add the cod's roes, dashi, soy sauce and mirin and continue to cook until the roes turn white. Stir in the leek and cook for a further 2 minutes.

4 Transfer the mixture to a warmed serving bowl and serve at once.

Sliced raw fish
(Sashimi)

Preparation:
40 minutes

Serves 2-4
1 lb firm fresh fish, filleted
1 tablespoon salt
Dipping sauce
2 teaspoons wasabi (Japanese horseradish mustard), mixed to a paste with water
½ cup soy sauce

1 Pat the fillets dry with absorbent kitchen paper and sprinkle the salt over them. Cover and put in the refrigerator for 30 minutes.

2 Remove the fish from the refrigerator and cut crosswise into bite-size pieces. Arrange the pieces on a large serving dish or on individual dishes.

3 Make the sauce. Mix the wasabi into the soy sauce, then pour the mixture into individual dipping bowls. The fish should be dipped in the sauce before eating.

● Sashimi is one of the finest and simplest of Japanese fish dishes. Almost any type of fish can be used – flounder, tuna, pompano, red, snapper or any type of shellfish – but it must be good quality and very fresh. To ensure freshness, it is better to buy a whole fish and have your fish man clean and fillet it for you.

If wished, dip the fish in boiling water to destroy any surface bacteria, then refresh under cold running water before sprinkling with salt.

Serve with a colorful garnish – try grated daikon mixed with chopped sweet red pepper.

Sliced raw fish (Sashimi)

Marinated salmon (Yok kai sake)

Marinated salmon
(Yok kai sake)

Preparation:
1¼ hours

Serves 4
*1 lb fresh salmon, thinly sliced
then cut in strips
1 inch piece of fresh gingerroot,
pared and chopped
1 garlic clove, crushed
2 scallions, chopped
1 teaspoon sugar
1 teaspoon salt
¼ cup soy sauce
⅔ cup sake*

1 Carefully arrange the salmon strips in a large, shallow serving dish.

2 Combine all the remaining ingredients in a bowl, beating until they are well mixed and the sugar has dissolved. Pour the mixture over the salmon strips and chill in the refrigerator for 1 hour.

3 Remove the salmon from the refrigerator and serve at once.

• Fresh spinach leaves and sprigs of herbs make attractive garnishes for this dish. Carrot flower shapes and slices of cucumber make excellent additional garnishes, to add a touch of color contrast.

Raw fish with vegetables (Sashimi to yasai)

Preparation:
30 minutes

Serves 6
1 lb flounder, filleted and skinned
For garnish
3 celery stalks, chopped
2 scallions, chopped
1 sweet red pepper, seeded and chopped
2 tablespoons soy sauce mixed with 2 teaspoons lemon juice
Dipping sauce
2 teaspoons wasabi (Japanese horseradish mustard) mixed to a paste with water
¼ cup soy sauce mixed with 2 tablespoons sake

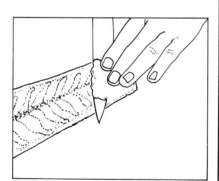

1 Place the flounder fillets in a colander and pour over boiling water. Refresh the fish under cold running water, then transfer to a chopping board. Cut the fillets, crosswise in very thin strips. Arrange the strips on a plate, cover with foil and chill in the refrigerator while arranging the garnish.

2 Put the vegetables in a small serving bowl and pour over the soy sauce mixture. Toss gently so that all the vegetable pieces are coated.

3 Remove the fish from the refrigerator and divide it between 6 individual serving bowls. Arrange a portion of the garnish on a plate beside each bowl.

4 Make the sauce. Stir the wasabi mixture into the soy sauce mixture and pour into individual dipping bowls.

5 Serve with the vegetable garnish. Dip the fish into the sauce before eating.

Marinated mackerel (Shimesaba)

Preparation:
2¼ hours

Serves 4
1 large mackerel, cleaned, gutted and filleted
1 teaspoon salt
2 cups white wine vinegar
For garnish
1½ inch piece of fresh gingerroot, pared and grated
4 scallions, minced
Dipping sauce
1 cup soy sauce
2 teaspoons wasabi (Japanese horseradish mustard), mixed to a paste with water

1 Sprinkle the mackerel fillets with salt and put into the refrigerator for 1 hour. Wash the fillets under cold running water and arrange in a shallow dish. Pour over the vinegar and leave for 1 hour, turning over at least once.

2 Remove the mackerel from the vinegar and pat dry on absorbent kitchen paper. Skin and remove any bones. Cut across each fillet at about 1 inch intervals and arrange the pieces decoratively on a serving dish. Garnish with the grated ginger and scallions.

3 Pour the soy sauce into individual dipping bowls and arrange the wasabi in individual small bowls. To make the dipping sauce, each person can mix soy sauce and wasabi to taste, then dip the fish into it.

Steamed fish with tofu
(Mushizakana to tofu tsukeawase)

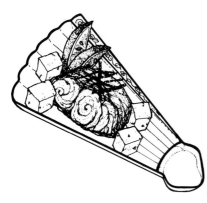

Preparation and cooking:
25 minutes

Serves 4
1 lb white fish fillets
1 cup tofu (bean curd) cut in
1 inch cubes
1 teaspoon salt
For garnish
¼ lb spinach, washed and drained
1 sheet of nori seaweed
1 lemon, cut in wedges or
decorative loops

1 Cut the fish in 8 pieces and divide among 4 small ovenproof dishes. Divide the tofu cubes among the dishes. Season each bowl with salt to taste.

2 Place each dish in the top part of a steamer or on an ovenproof plate. Fill the base of the steamer (or a medium saucepan over which the plate will fit) about two-thirds full of boiling water and fit the top part over. Cover and steam for 10 minutes.

3 Meanwhile, cook the spinach. Put spinach in a saucepan with only the water that clings to the leaves. Cover the saucepan and cook over medium heat for about 5 minutes until the spinach is soft and tender. Drain, rinse under cold water and drain again. Cut in wedges.

4 Preheat the broiler to medium high. Place the nori sheet on the broiler rack; broil until crisp on both sides.

5 Garnish the steamed fish and tofu with the spinach and lemon wedges. Crumble over the nori and serve.

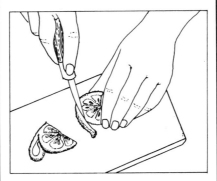

● To make lemon loops for the garnish, cut the lemon in slices, then halve the slices. Cut around each half slice, between the peel and pith, to within ½ inch of the end. Curl the peel under to make a loop.

Overleaf: Steamed fish with tofu
(Mushizakana to tofu tsukeawase)

Steamed fish with daikon and egg
(*Mushizakana to daikon to tamago tsukeawase*)

Preparation and cooking:
30 minutes

Serves 4
1 lb white fish fillets
1 teaspoon salt
2 tablespoons sake
1 egg
1 teaspoon sugar
1 cup grated daikon (Japanese
white radish) or icicle radish
4 young spinach leaves
1 inch piece of fresh gingerroot,
pared and grated

1 Cut the fish in 8 pieces and divide among 4 small ovenproof dishes. Season each bowl with salt and sprinkle a little sake over each portion of fish, using a total of 1 tablespoon.

2 Combine the egg, sugar, daikon and remaining sake and divide the mixture among the 4 dishes. Garnish each with a spinach leaf.

3 Place each dish in the top part of a steamer or on an ovenproof plate. Fill the base of the steamer (or a medium saucepan over which the plate will fit) about two-thirds full of boiling water and fit the top part over. Cover and steam for 12-15 minutes or until the egg has set.

4 Remove from the steamer, sprinkle with grated ginger and serve at once.

Glazed shrimp
(*Kimini*)

Preparation and cooking:
20 minutes

Serves 2-4
12 jumbo shrimp, body shell
removed and tails left intact
½ cup cornstarch
3½ tablespoons dashi (Japanese
stock),
see page 10
2 tablespoons sake
½ teaspoon sugar
¼ teaspoon salt
3 egg yolks, well beaten

1 Dip the shrimp into the cornstarch, then shake off any excess.

2 Bring a saucepan of water to a boil, add the shrimp and cook for about 10 seconds. Remove with a slotted spoon or chopsticks and rinse under cold running water. Set aside.

3 Pour the dashi into a small saucepan and stir in the sake, sugar and salt. Bring to the boil. Place the shrimp in the pan and return the liquid to a boil, basting the shrimp.

4 When the liquid boils, pour the beaten egg yolks slowly over the shrimp. Do not stir. Reduce the heat, cover the pan and simmer for 2 minutes. Remove from the heat and let stand for a further 2 minutes before serving.

Broiled squid
(Ika no tsukeyaki)

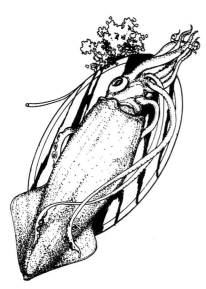

Preparation and cooking:
30 minutes

Serves 4
4 medium squid, cleaned
Marinade
⅔ cup soy sauce
⅔ cup sake
2 tablespoons sugar
For garnish
4 tablespoons grated daikon
(Japanese white radish)

1 Remove the tentacles from the squid, then rub away the outer skin. Set aside.

2 Put the soy sauce, sake and sugar into a small saucepan and bring to a boil. Remove the pan from the heat and pour the mixture into a large shallow dish. Arrange the squid in the dish and leave to marinate at room temperature for 15 minutes.

3 Preheat the broiler to medium.

4 Remove the squid from the marinade and pat dry with absorbent kitchen paper. Reserve the marinade. Score the surface of the squid and arrange them on the broiler rack. Broil for 8 minutes on each side, basting occasionally with the marinating liquid.

5 Remove the squid to a chopping board and cut in strips about 1 inch wide. Arrange decoratively on a serving platter and pour over the remaining marinade. Garnish with grated daikon and serve at once.

Shrimp with bamboo shoots
(Takenoko-iri ebi no umani)

Preparation and cooking:
15 minutes

Serves 4
¼ cup water
¼ cup soy sauce
2 cups shelled shrimp
1 can (16 oz) bamboo shoots,
drained and sliced
2 tablespoons sake
2 tablespoons mirin (sweet rice
wine)

1 Put the water and soy sauce into a shallow saucepan and bring to a boil. Reduce the heat to medium and stir in the shrimp. Cook for 5 minutes. Using a slotted spoon, transfer the shrimp to a warmed bowl and keep hot.

2 Add the bamboo shoot slices to the pan and return to a boil. Stir in the sake and mirin and cook for 3 minutes. Return the shrimp to the pan and stir the mixture well. Cook for 1 minute.

3 Transfer the shrimp mixture to a warmed serving dish and serve at once.

Tempura

Preparation and cooking:
45 minutes

Serves 4
*12 jumbo shrimp, body shell
removed and tails left on
4 mushrooms, stems removed
1 large carrot, cut in sticks
1 large green pepper, seeded and
cut in 8 pieces
1 onion, cut in ¼ inch slices
vegetable oil for deep-frying*
Sauce
*⅔ cup dashi (Japanese stock), see
page 10
2 tablespoons soy sauce
pinch of salt
2 teaspoons sugar
⅔ cup finely grated daikon
(Japanese white radish)*
Batter
*1 egg, lightly beaten
¾ cup water
1 cup flour, sifted*

1 Make the sauce. Stir together all the ingredients except the daikon in a small saucepan. Bring to a boil, remove from the heat and set aside.

2 Make the batter. Place the beaten egg and water in a medium-size bowl and beat lightly. Add the flour all in one go and mix lightly with chopsticks — it will be lumpy.

3 Fill a deep, heavy-bottomed saucepan with oil to a depth of 3¼ inches and heat to 350°F.

4 Quickly dip the ingredients in the batter and cook in batches, starting with the vegetables, until puffed and golden. Add only enough ingredients at once to cover half the surface of the oil; if too many are fried at once, the temperature of the oil is lowered and the food will not cook properly.

5 Drain on a rack or absorbent kitchen paper, then transfer to individual plates.

6 Stir the daikon into the sauce in the pan, pour into 4 individual small bowls and serve at once with the tempura.

- Tempura is one of the best known Japanese dishes outside Japan, although it is not traditionally Japanese, but rather an adaptation of a Portugese dish. The name comes from the Latin word for time.
- In Japan, plates or racks of meshed bamboo are often used for serving tempura. The meshed bamboo is usually lined with special absorbent tempura paper which is sold ready-cut to size in packages.
- Tempura is best eaten as soon as it is cooked, so be sure to have everything ready to serve before starting to cook.

Tempura

Eggs with shrimp and peas
(*Iri-tamago*)

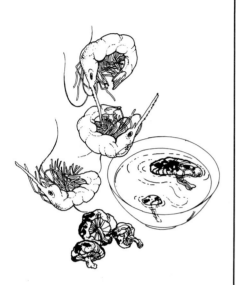

Preparation and cooking:
40 minutes

Serves 2-3
3 dried shiitake mushrooms
4 eggs, lightly beaten
¼ cup dashi (Japanese stock), see
page 10
1 teaspoon sugar
2 teaspoons soy sauce
2 teaspoons sake
3 tablespoons vegetable oil
⅔ cup frozen shelled baby
shrimp, thawed
1¼ cups frozen peas, thawed

1 Soak the dried shiitake mushrooms in lukewarm water for 20 minutes. Drain, then trim the stems and slice the mushrooms.

2 Beat the eggs, dashi, sugar, soy sauce and sake together until they are thoroughly mixed. Set aside.

3 Heat the oil in a large skillet, add the shrimp, peas and mushrooms and stir-fry for 3-4 minutes, or until the shrimp and peas are cooked through.

4 Stir in the egg mixture and reduce the heat to medium low. Cook, stirring occasionally, until the egg has just lightly set.

5 Carefully transfer to a warmed serving dish and serve at once.

Sake and soy-flavored clams
(*Hamaguri shigure-ni*)

Preparation and cooking:
30 minutes

Serves 4
½ cup sake
¼ cup sugar
12 shucked littleneck clams,
¼ cup soy sauce

1 In a large, heavy skillet, combine the sake, sugar and clams. Stir the mixture thoroughly with a wooden spoon. Bring to a boil and cook for 3 minutes, stirring constantly.

2 Stir in the soy sauce and boil for 1 minute, stirring constantly. Using a slotted spoon or chopsticks, transfer the clams to a plate.

3 Boil the sauce for another 10 minutes, or until it becomes thick and rather syrupy. Return the clams to the pan and stir them gently into the sauce. Cook the mixture for about 1 minute, or until the clams are thoroughly coated with the sauce.

4 Remove from the heat and spoon the mixture into a warmed serving dish. Serve at once.

Vegetables and seafood with rice
(Mazezushi)

Preparation and cooking:
2 hours

Serves 6
2¼ cups short-grain rice
2½ cups water
Vinegar sauce
¼ cup white wine vinegar
1 tablespoon sugar
½ teaspoon salt
Vegetables
4 dried shiitake mushrooms
2 carrots, thinly sliced
1 canned bamboo shoot, drained
and thinly sliced
¼ small turnip, thinly sliced
3 tablespoons frozen peas
¾ cup dashi (Japanese stock), see
page 10
1 tablespoon sake
1 tablespoon sugar
1 tablespoon vegetable oil
2 tablespoons soy sauce
Omelet
1 tablespoon vegetable oil
3 eggs, lightly beaten
Seafood
⅔ cup cooked, shelled shrimp
⅔ cup flaked crabmeat, free of
cartilage

1 Soak and cook the rice following the instructions for Plain boiled rice (see page 62).

2 Transfer the drained rice to a warmed bowl and set aside.

3 Make the vinegar sauce. Combine all the ingredients and pour over the rice. Stir gently with a wooden spoon and let cool at room temperature.

4 Meanwhile, prepare the vegetables. Soak the dried mushrooms in lukewarm water for 20 minutes. Drain, trim the stems and slice the mushrooms.

5 Put the carrots, bamboo shoot, turnip and peas into a saucepan and pour over enough water to cover. Bring to a boil and cook briskly for 2 minutes. Drain.

6 Put ½ cup of the dashi, the sake and half the sugar in a small saucepan and bring to a boil. Add the drained vegetables and cook for a further 2 minutes. Transfer the vegetables to a bowl with a slotted spoon and reserve the dashi liquid.

7 Heat the oil in a small skillet, then add the mushrooms, remaining dashi and sugar, and the soy sauce. Cook, stirring constantly, for 3 minutes. Remove from the heat and cool.

8 Make the omelet. Brush an omelet pan or 8 inch skillet with oil and heat. Pour in about one-third of the egg mixture and tilt the pan so that the mixture covers the base of the pan, then leave to cook until the omelet has set. Shake the pan slightly to loosen the omelet, then turn over and cook the other side for 15 seconds. Slide onto a plate and cook two more omelets in the same way. When all the omelets have been cooked, pile them on top of one another and cut in thin strips.

9 To assemble, stir the vegetables and reserved cooking liquid gently into the vinegared rice with a wooden spoon. Stir in the shrimp and crabmeat. Arrange the egg strips decoratively over the top and serve at once.

Seafood tempura

Preparation and cooking:
1 hour

Serves 4
1 eggplant
salt
8 jumbo shrimp, body shells
removed and tails left on
2 small squid, cleaned
½ lb haddock fillet, skinned
and cut in fingers
½ sweet potato, weighing about
¼ lb pared and sliced
1 carrot, cut in ⅛ inch
slices
4 green beans, trimmed and cut in
2 inch lengths
4 scallions
vegetable oil for deep-frying
soy sauce for dipping
Batter
1 egg
¾ cup water
1 cup flour

Seafood tempura

1 Cut the eggplant lengthwise into 8 slices, about ¼ inch thick, discarding the end slices. Cut each slice into quarters. Put the slices in a colander, sprinkle with salt and let drain for 30 minutes. Rinse the slices and dry well on absorbent kitchen paper.

2 Interlink the shrimp head to tail in pairs to make a circle. Secure each pair with a cocktail pick.

3 Cut the squid flesh in rings.

4 Arrange the seafood and vegetables on a tray.

5 Fill a small heavy-bottomed saucepan with oil to a depth of 3¼ inches and heat to 350°F.

6 Meanwhile, make the batter. Place the beaten egg and water in a medium-size bowl and beat lightly. Add the flour, all at once, and mix lightly with chopsticks — it will be lumpy.

7 Quickly dip the ingredients in the batter and cook in batches, starting with the vegetables, until puffed and golden. Add only enough ingredients at once to cover half the surface of the oil; if too many are fried at once, the temperature of the oil is lowered and the food will not cook properly.

8 Drain on a rack or absorbent kitchenpaper, then transfer to individual plates.

9 Pour the soy sauce into 4 small bowls and serve at once with the tempura.

Sake-flavored clams
(Hamaguri sakamushi)

Preparation and cooking:
50 minutes

Serves 4
¼ cup sake
12 shucked littleneck clams, half
the shells scrubbed and reserved
For garnish
12 lemon slices

1 Put the sake into a large saucepan and bring to a boil. Add the clams, stirring with a wooden spoon. Cover the pan, reduce the heat and simmer over low heat for 5 minutes.

2 Using a slotted spoon or chopsticks, remove the clams and arrange 1 on each of the reserved shells. Garnish each shell with a lemon slice.

3 Arrange the clams on a serving dish and let cool at room temperature, then chill in the refrigerator for 30 minutes before serving.

Sake-flavoured clams (Hamaguri sakamushi)

Crab and cucumber with vinegar dressing
(Kani no sunomono)

Preparation:
1¼ hours

Serves 2
½ cucumber
salt
1¼ cups flaked crabmeat
Vinegar dressing
2 tablespoons white wine vinegar
2 tablespoons mirin (sweet rice wine)
2 tablespoons dashi (Japanese stock), see page 10
1 tablespoon soy sauce
2 teaspoons sugar

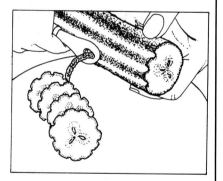

1 Partially pare the cucumber, leaving some long green strips for color. Slice as thinly as possible, arrange in a colander and sprinkle with salt. Let drain for about 30 minutes. Squeeze out any excess liquid, then pat dry on absorbent kitchen paper.

2 Arrange the cucumber and prepared crabmeat decoratively in a shallow dish.

3 Make the vinegar dressing. Combine all the ingredients, beating until they are well blended. Pour the dressing over the cucumber and crabmeat and toss gently so that they are well coated. Leave to marinate at room temperature for 30 minutes, tossing gently occasionally.

4 Carefully drain off any excess dressing and serve.

Deep-fried shrimp and green pepper
(Ebi to pimen no agemono)

Preparation and cooking:
20 minutes

Serves 4
12 jumbo shrimp, body shells removed and tails left on
cornstarch for dusting
1 egg white, lightly beaten
1½ cups fresh white bread crumbs
2 green peppers, seeded and cut into ½ inch thick strips
vegetable oil for deep-frying

1 Dust the shrimp with cornstarch, then brush with egg white and finally roll in the bread crumbs to coat well.

2 Fill a deep, heavy-bottomed saucepan with oil to a depth of 3¼ inches and heat to 350°F. Cook a few of the shrimp for 1-2 minutes. Remove with a slotted spoon or chopsticks, drain on absorbent kitchen paper and keep warm while cooking the remainder.

3 Deep fry the pepper strips for 1 minute.

4 Arrange the shrimp and the peppers in small bowls and serve at once.

Broiled crab wrapped in seaweed
(Yakigani no norimaki)

Preparation and cooking:
45 minutes

Serves 4
1 cup canned crabmeat
2 tablespoons minced fresh parsley
¼ teaspoon salt
1 egg, beaten
2 sheets of nori seaweed
For garnish
thin slices of cucumber

1 Put the crabmeat, parsley, salt and egg in a bowl and mash together. Cut each sheet of nori into 4 x ½ inch squares.

2 Preheat the broiler to high.

3 Spoon the crabmeat mixture onto the pieces of nori and wrap them up as tightly as possible without tearing the nori. Place the packages, seam side down, on a very lightly greased baking sheet.

4 Broil the nori packages for about 3 minutes on the top side only. Remove from the heat, let cool slightly, then cut each package in half.

5 Arrange the packages on a serving platter, garnish with cucumber slices and serve.

● The packages may be deep-fried instead of broiled – dip the packages in beaten egg, dust with cornstarch and deep fry at 350° until crisp.

Oysters and seaweed with miso
(Kaki to wakame no nuta)

Preparation and cooking:
20 minutes

Serves 3-4
1 tablespoon wakame seaweed
1 pint shucked Olympia oysters, washed
1 celery stalk, chopped
8 scallions, chopped
Miso sauce
2½ tablespoons white wine vinegar
2½ tablespoons sake
2½ tablespoons sugar
5 tablespoons miso (bean paste)

1 Soak the wakame seaweed in water until soft. Drain.

2 Meanwhile, make the sauce. Put the vinegar, sake and sugar into a saucepan and bring to a boil. Off heat, stir in the miso until it melts. Pour into individual dipping bowls and set aside.

3 Chop the wakame, then arrange with the remaining ingredients on a large serving platter or individual serving plates. The sauce can be mixed into the ingredients or passed separately.

Rice

Amongst the attractive array of dishes that make up a Japanese meal, rice is sure to be featured. Plain boiled rice is the perfect accompaniment to all meat, seafood and vegetable dishes, but it can also form the basis of many interesting complete dishes. The Japanese artistic sense is illustrated in the classic garnished rice patties and seaweed-wrapped rice rolls, while unusual combinations of rice with tea or spinach are inspirational.

Plain boiled rice
(Gohan)

Preparation and cooking:
1 hour

Serves 4-6
2¼ cups short-grain rice
2½ cups water

1 Rinse the rice several times until the rinsing water is clear. Put the rice in a bowl, cover with fresh water and let soak for about 20 minutes.

2 Drain the rice and put in a saucepan. Pour over the water, then bring to a boil.

3 Cover the pan, reduce the heat to low and simmer for 15-20 minutes, or until the rice is cooked and the liquid has been absorbed.

4 Reduce the heat to an absolute minimum and leave for 15 minutes. Turn off the heat but let the saucepan stand on the range for a further 10 minutes.

5 Transfer to a warmed serving bowl. The rice is now ready to serve.

● The cooked rice should be slightly sticky in texture.

Rice patties topped with raw fish (Nigiri zushi)

Rice patties topped with raw fish
(*Nigiri zushi*)

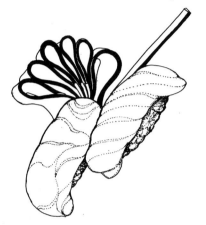

Preparation and cooking:
2½ hours

Serves 4
2 cups short-grain rice
3 inch square of kombu seaweed,
cut in a
½ inch fringe
2 cups water
¼ cup rice vinegar
1 tablespoon sugar
2 teaspoons salt
Topping
1 teaspoon rice vinegar
4 fresh large uncooked shrimp
4 fresh sea scallops
¼ lb fresh sea bass, sea bream or
tuna
1 tablespoon wasabi (Japanese
horseradish mustard), mixed to a
paste with water
4 tablespoons red caviar, real or
mock
¼ lb salmon roes
For garnish
sliced tomato, cut radishes,
cucumber strips, scallion tassels
soy sauce

1 Soak the rice following the directions for Plain boiled rice (see page 62).

2 Put the rice into a heavy-bottomed saucepan with a tightly fitting lid. Bury the kombu seaweed in the rice. Add the water, cover and bring to a boil over high heat. Remove the kombu just before the water boils and reserve.

3 Reduce the heat to medium and cook for 5-6 minutes, then reduce the heat to very low and cook for 15 minutes.

4 Raise the heat to high for 10 seconds, then remove the pan from the heat. Let the rice stand for 10 minutes.

5 Combine the vinegar, sugar and salt in a small saucepan over medium heat and heat through. Turn the rice out into a large shallow dish, preferably wooden. Gradually pour the vinegar mixture over the rice, mixing it with a wooden spatula or a fork, and fanning it vigorously at the same time. Fanning cools the rice quickly and makes it glisten.

6 When the rice is cool, wet the hands with water to which a little rice vinegar has been added, and form the rice into about 24 oblong patties, 1 x 2 inches.

7 Prepare the topping. Bring a small pan of salted water to a boil. Add the vinegar and the shrimp, reduce the heat and simmer the shrimp for 1 minute. Drain.

8 When the shrimp are cool enough to handle, shell and drain them. Cut the undersides from end to end three-fourths of the way through, then turn the shrimp over and flatten them.

9 Slice the sea scallop corals in 2 horizontally. Slice the discs in 3 horizontally. Slice the raw fish diagonally in slices ¼ in thick.

10 Spread a dab of wasabi down the center of each piece of fish and lay it, wasabi side down, on top of some of the patties. Spread the salmon roes directly on some of the patties and put a dab of wasabi on top of the roes. Arrange the shrimp on more patties and the red caviar on the remainder. Arrange the kombu fringe on the side of some patties. Garnish with the sliced tomato, radishes, cucumber and scallion tassels.

11 Fill a small bowl with soy sauce and serve with the patties. To eat, use chopsticks or fingers to dip the patties in the soy sauce.

● This dish is usually served as a snack or appetizer in Japan.

Chicken with eggs and rice
(Oyako donburi)

Preparation and cooking:
1 hour

Serves 4
2¼ cups short-grain rice
2½ cups water
3 tablespoons vegetable oil
2 small chicken breasts, skinned,
boned and cut in thin strips
2 onions, thinly sliced
4 eggs, lightly beaten
2 sheets of nori seaweed
Sauce
¼ cup water
¼ cup soy sauce
¼ cup dashi (Japanese stock), see
page 10

1 Soak and cook the rice following the directions for Plain boiled rice (see page 62).

2 Meanwhile, heat the oil in a skillet, add the chicken pieces and cook until they are just cooked through. Remove from the heat and transfer to a plate using a slotted spoon or chopsticks.

3 Combine the sauce ingredients in a bowl. Put one-fourth of the sauce mixture into a small skillet and bring to a boil. Add about one-fourth of the onions and sauté briskly for 3 minutes. Add one-fourth of the chicken slices and one-fourth of the beaten egg. Reduce the heat to low and stir once. Leave until the egg has set, then cover the pan and steam for 1 minute.

4 Spoon about one-fourth of the rice unto an individual serving bowl and top with the egg mixture. Repeat this process 3 more times, using up the remaining ingredients.

5 Meanwhile, preheat the broiler to medium high. Place the nori on the broiler rack and broil until it is crisp. Remove from the heat and crumble over the rice and egg mixture. Serve at once.

Chestnut rice
(Kuri gohan)

Preparation and cooking:
1¾ hours

Serves 4-6
2¼ cups short-grain rice
1 lb chestnuts
2½ cups water
1½ tablespoons sake
1 teaspoon salt

1 Rinse the rice several times until the water runs clear. Put the rice in a bowl, cover with fresh water and let soak for 30 minutes.

2 Meanwhile, put the chestnuts into a saucepan and pour over water to cover. Bring to a boil, then reduce the heat and simmer for 15 minutes. Drain and remove the skins from the chestnuts. Leave whole, or quarter them if they are large.

3 Drain the rice and put into a saucepan with the chestnuts, water, sake and salt and cook following the instructions for Plain boiled rice (see page 62). Serve at once.

• If wished, substitute canned chestnuts for the fresh chestnuts; the pre-cooking can be omitted and the chestnuts added straight to the rice.

Meat on rice
(Niku donburi)

Preparation and cooking:
1 hour

Serves 4
2¼ cups short-grain rice
2½ cups water
½ lb beef fillet, trimmed and
thinly sliced
2 tablespoons sesame oil
4 scallions, thinly sliced
1 green pepper, seeded and sliced
lengthwise
2 thin slices of fresh gingerroot,
pared and cut in thin strips
1 cup diced thinly sliced ham
2 slices of bacon, diced
Marinade
⅓ cup soy sauce
⅓ cup dashi (Japanese stock), see
page 10
1 tablespoon sugar
For garnish
4 scallion tassels

1 Soak and cook the rice following the directions given for Plain boiled rice (see page 62).

2 Meanwhile, make the marinade. Combine the soy sauce, dashi and sugar together in a shallow bowl. Add the beef slices and leave to marinate at room temperature for 15 minutes, basting occasionally. Remove from the marinade and pat dry with absorbent kitchen paper. Reserve the marinade.

3 Heat the oil in a large skillet. Add the sliced scallions, green pepper and strips of ginger and sauté for 1-2 minutes, stirring.

4 Add the diced ham, bacon and beef slices and continue to sauté for 6-7 minutes, stirring constantly. Stir in the reserved marinade and heat through.

5 Transfer the cooked rice to a serving plate or individual serving bowls. Spoon the meat mixture over the rice, garnish with scallion tassels and serve at once.

Meat on rice (Niku donburi)

Fried rice and bamboo shoots
(*Takenoko-iri yaki-meshi*)

Preparation and cooking:
1¼ hours

Serves 3-4
1¼ cups short-grain rice
1¼ cups water
¾ cup canned bamboo shoots
2 tablespoons vegetable oil
2 scallions, chopped
3 tablespoons minced
fresh parsley
grated rind of 1 lemon
2 tablespoons soy sauce
shichimi togarashi

1 Soak and cook the rice following the directions given for Plain boiled rice (see page 62).

2 Meanwhile, drain the bamboo shoots, reserving the can juice in a small saucepan. Slice the bamboo shoots, add to the pan of can juice and bring to a boil. Boil for 10 minutes, then drain.

3 Heat the oil in a skillet, add the chopped scallions and parsley and sauté briskly, stirring, for 2 minutes.

4 Add the rice, bamboo shoots, lemon rind, soy sauce and shichimi togarashi to taste to the pan. Stir gently until heated through, then serve at once.

Pork scallops with rice
(*Katsudon*)

Preparation and cooking:
1 hour

Serves 4
2½ cups short-grain rice
2¼ cups water
4 eggs, lightly beaten
½ cup flour
¾ cup dried bread crumbs
1¼ lb pork tenderloin, cut in
4 scallops
vegetable oil for deep-frying
3 cups dashi (Japanese stock), see
page 12
⅔ cup soy sauce
1½ tablespoons mirin (sweet rice
wine)
2 onions, thinly sliced in rings

1 Soak and cook the rice following the directions given for Plain boiled rice (see page 62).

2 Meanwhile, put half the beaten egg, flour and bread crumbs into separate bowls. Dip the pork scallops first in the beaten egg, then in the flour and finally in the dried bread crumbs, coating thoroughly and shaking off any excess.

3 Fill a large, heavy-bottomed saucepan one-third full with oil and heat until very hot. Carefully lower the scallops, 2 at a time, into the oil and fry until they are golden brown. Drain on absorbent kitchen paper. Set aside and keep hot.

4 Put the dashi, soy sauce and mirin into a saucepan and bring to a boil. Reduce the heat to low, add the onion rings and simmer for 10 minutes, or until the rings are soft.

5 Slice the pork in thin strips and add to the pan. Pour in the remaining beaten egg and simmer the mixture gently for 3 minutes. Remove from the heat.

6 Transfer the cooked rice to individual serving bowls. Top with the egg, onion and pork mixture and pour over any remaining liquid from the pan. Serve at once.

Red cooked rice
(Seki han)

Preparation and cooking:
soaking, then 1½ hours

Serves 3-4
*1⅔ cups dried azuki beans,
soaked overnight in cold water
2 cups short-grain rice
1 teaspoon salt
2 tablespoons sake
1 tablespoon soy sauce*

1 Rinse the beans, put in a saucepan and cover with fresh water. Bring to a boil and boil briskly for a few minutes, then reduce the heat and cook over low heat for 1 hour, or until the beans are just tender.

2 Meanwhile, soak the rice following the directions given for Plain boiled rice (see page 62).

3 Remove the pan of beans from the heat and drain, reserving the cooking liquid. Transfer the beans to a bowl and keep hot.

4 Cook the rice following the directions on page 62, except that instead of using all water to cook the rice, use the bean cooking liquid and make up any extra liquid needed with water.

5 About 5 minutes before the rice is ready to serve, stir in the reserved beans, the salt, sake and soy sauce and cook until heated through.

6 Transfer the mixture to a warmed serving bowl and serve at once.

Chicken and rice
(Oboro)

Preparation and cooking:
1 hour

Serves 4-6
*2¼ cups short-grain rice
2 ½ cups water
6 dried shiitake mushrooms
⅓ cup soy sauce
⅓ cup sake
1 teaspoon sugar
2 chicken breasts, skinned, boned
and cut in strips
1⅓ cup frozen peas
4 eggs beaten
½ cup dashi (Japanese stock), see
page 10
pinch of salt
1 tablespoon vegetable oil*

1 Soak and cook the rice following the directions given for Plain boiled rice (see page 62).

2 Meanwhile, soak the mushrooms in lukewarm water for 20 minutes, then drain. Remove the stems from the mushrooms and cook the caps in boiling water for 5 minutes, drain, then cut in slices. Set aside.

3 Put the soy sauce, sake and sugar into a large saucepan and bring to a boil, stirring constantly until the sugar has dissolved. Add the chicken strips and peas to the pan and reduce the heat to low. Cover and simmer for 10 minutes, or until the chicken strips are cooked. Remove from the heat and set aside.

4 Heat a rectangular omelet pan (makiyaki-nabe) or an 8 inch heavy-bottomed skillet pan, and add just enough oil to coat the surface.

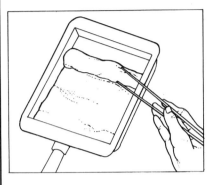

5 Combine the beaten egg with the dashi and salt, then pour about a third of the egg mixture into the pan and tilt the pan to cover the whole surface. When set, carefully roll up the omelet toward you, then slide to the far side of the pan.

6 Brush the pan with more oil and, when hot, pour in half the remaining egg mixture. Gently lift the rolled omelet so that the new egg covers the whole surface of pan. Cook again until the omelet is set, then roll up the second omelet as before, enclosing the first omelet within the second one Repeat with remaining egg mixture.

7 Carefully slide the rolled omelet onto a plate and cut in thin slices.

8 When the rice is cooked, transfer to a warmed serving bowl. Arrange the chicken strips and peas on top and pour over the chicken cooking liquid. Scatter over the mushrooms and omelet slices and serve at once.

Rice salad with fish
(Chirashi zushi)

**Preparation and cooking:
2¾ hours**

Serves 4-6
*1 small mackerel, cleaned, gutted
and filleted
salt
2 cups white wine vinegar
1 cup sliced green beans
2 sheets of nori seaweed
1 small piece of fresh gingerroot,
pared and cut in needle shreds*
Rice
*2¼ cups short-grain rice
2½ cups water
⅓ cup white wine vinegar
1½ tablespoons sugar
1 tablespoon salt*
Kanpyo
*handful of kanpyo (dried gourd)
3 tablespoons soy sauce
2 tablespoons sugar
1 cup water*
Mushrooms
*5 dried shiitake mushrooms
2 cups lukewarm water
1½ tablespoons soy sauce
3 tablespoons sugar
1½ tablespoons sake
½ teaspoon salt*
Carrots
*1 large carrot, sliced
2 teaspoon sugar
¼ teaspoon salt*
Omelet
*4 eggs, lightly beaten
½ cup dashi (Japanese stock), see
page 10
few drops of soy sauce
½ teaspoon salt
1 tablespoon vegetable oil*

1 Sprinkle the mackerel fillets with 1 tablespoon salt and chill in the refrigerator for 1 hour. Remove from the refrigerator then soak in the vinegar for 1 hour.

Rice salad with fish (Chirashi zushi)

2 Meanwhile, soak and cook the rice following the directions for Plain boiled rice (see page 62). Soak the kanpyo in cold water for 1 hour, then drain. Soak the shiitake mushrooms in the lukewarm water for 20 minutes, then drain, reserving the liquid. Remove the stems and slice the mushrooms.

3 Transfer the rice to a warm bowl and set aside. To make the vinegar sauce for the rice, combine the vinegar, sugar and salt, then pour the mixture over the rice. Stir gently with a wooden spoon and set aside to cool at room temperature.

4 Remove the mackerel fillets from the vinegar and pat dry on absorbent kitchen paper. Cut vertically in thin strips and set aside.

5 Cook the beans in boiling salted water for 5 minutes, or until they are just tender. Drain and set aside.

6 Preheat the broiler to medium high. Place the nori sheets on the broil rack and broil until crisp on both sides. Remove from the heat and set aside.

7 Prepare the kanpyo. Put the kanpyo into a saucepan and add just enough water to cover. Bring to a boil and cook briskly until tender. Drain, then return to the saucepan with the soy sauce, sugar and water. Cook over medium heat for 10 minutes, to ensure that the flavors are absorbed by the kanpyo. Set the kanpyo aside.

8 Make the mushroom mixture. Put the mushroom draining liquid in a small saucepan and add the soy sauce, sugar, sake and salt. Stir in the mushroom pieces and bring to a boil. Cook over medium heat for 15 minutes, then transfer the mushrooms to a plate with a slotted spoon. Add the carrots to the saucepan with the sugar and salt. Reduce the heat to low and simmer until all the sauce has evaporated. Remove from the heat and set aside.

9 Make the omelet. Beat the eggs, dashi and soy sauce together. Heat a rectangular omelet pan (makiyaki-nabe), or an 8 inch skillet, and add just enough oil to coat the surface.

10 Add a third of the egg mixture and tilt the pan so the egg covers the whole surface. When set, roll up the omelet toward you, then slide to the end of pan.

11 Brush the pan with more oil and, when hot, pour in another third of egg mixture. Gently lift the rolled omelet so that the new egg covers the whole surface of the pan. Cook until set, then roll up as before, enclosing the first omelet within the second one. Repeat with remaining egg mixture, then cut the roll into thin slices.

12 To assemble, arrange the rice in a large serving bowl. Combine the mushrooms, carrots and kanpyo and stir gently into the rice. Arrange the beans, egg strips and sliced mackerel on top and sprinkle over the ginger. Crumble over the nori and serve at once.

Rice rolls wrapped in seaweed
(*Nori maki*)

Preparation and cooking:
2½ hours

Serves 8
1 tablespoon kanpyo (dried gourd strips)
salt
2 small mackerel fillets
⅔ cup white wine vinegar
4½ cups short-grain rice
5 cups water
1 tablespoon soy sauce
¼ cup water
2 teaspoons sugar
½ cucumber
4 oz fresh tuna
4 sheets of nori seaweed
1 tablespoon wasabi (Japanese horseradish mustard), mixed to a paste with water
1½ cups soy sauce
Vinegar sauce
½ cup white wine vinegar
1½ tablespoons sugar
1½ teaspoons salt

1 Soak the kanpyo in cold salted water for 1 hour, then drain thoroughly. Soak the mackerel in the vinegar for 1 hour.

2 Meanwhile, soak and cook the rice following the directions for Plain boiled rice (see page 62) but using 5 cups water. Drain the rice and transfer to a warmed serving bowl.

3 Make the vinegar sauce. Combine the vinegar, sugar and salt, then pour the mixture over the rice. Stir gently with a wooden spoon and set aside to cool at room temperature.

4 Put the kanpyo into a saucepan and just cover with water. Bring to a boil and cook briskly until it is just tender. Drain, then return the kanpyo to the saucepan and add the soy sauce, water and sugar. Cook over moderate heat for 10 minutes to ensure that the flavors are absorbed by the kanpyo. Set aside.

5 Remove the mackerel from the vinegar and pat dry on absorbent kitchen paper. Cut the flesh vertically into long strips. Slice the cucumber and tuna into long thin strips, about the same length as the nori. Set aside.

6 Preheat the broiler to medium high. Place the nori sheets on the broiler rack and broil until crisp on 1 side. Remove from the heat and cut each sheet in half lengthwise.

7 Place a halved nori sheet on a bamboo mat (sudare) or heavy cloth napkin. Spread a handful of the rice over the nori to within about 2 inches of the edges. Smear a little wasabi over the rice. Arrange 2 or 3 strips of mackerel across the centre of the rice.

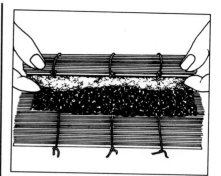

8 Roll up the mat or napkin gently, but firmly, to form a long cylinder. Repeat this process with the remaining mackerel. Continue to make cylinders in the same way using the kanpyo, cucumber and tuna instead of the mackerel. Omit the wasabi from the kanpyo cylinders.

9 When all the cylinders have been formed, gently slice across them to form sections about 1 inch wide.

10 Pour the soy sauce into small, individual dipping bowls and dip the nori sections into the sauce before eating.

● If fresh tuna is unavailable, double the amount of mackerel used.

Chicken kabob with rice
(Yakitori donburi)

Preparation and cooking:
1½ hours

Serves 4-6
1 lb chicken breast, skinned,
boned and cut into 1 inch cubes
2¼ cups short-grain rice
2½ cups water
Marinade
2 tablespoons soy sauce
1 tablespoon sugar
1 garlic clove, crushed
Sauce
2 tablespoons mirin (sweet rice
wine)
1 tablespoon soy sauce
½ cup dashi (Japanese stock), see
page 10

1 Combine all the marinade ingredients in a large dish. Add the chicken cubes, turn to coat and leave to marinate at room temperature for 1 hour.

2 Meanwhile, soak and cook the rice following the directions for Plain boiled rice (see page 62).

3 Preheat the broiler to medium high. Thread the marinated chicken cubes onto 4-6 skewers, then broil for about 15 minutes, turning occasionally to ensure even cooking.

4 Meanwhile, make the sauce. Combine the ingredients in a small saucepan and bring to a boil. Reduce the heat and simmer for 5 minutes.

5 To serve, arrange the cooked rice in a large dish, arrange the skewers of chicken on the top and pour over the sauce.

Fish and rice
(Sashimi gohan)

Preparation and cooking:
2½ hours

Serves 4
1 large mackerel, cleaned, gutted
and filleted
1 teaspoon salt
2 cups white wine vinegar
2¼ cups short-grain rice
2½ cups water
For garnish
1½ inch piece of fresh gingerroot,
pared and grated
5 scallions, minced
Dipping Sauce
1½ cups soy sauce
2 teaspoons wasabi (Japanese
horseradish mustard), mixed to a
paste with water

1 Sprinkle the mackerel fillets with salt and chill in the refrigerator for 1 hour. Remove from the refrigerator and soak in the vinegar for a further 1 hour.

2 Meanwhile, soak and cook the rice following the directions for Plain boiled rice (see page 62). Remove from the heat and transfer to a warmed serving bowl. Set aside and keep hot.

3 Remove the fish from the vinegar and pat dry with absorbent kitchen paper. Cut vertically in 1½ inch pieces, removing any bones.

4 Arrange the fish decoratively on a serving platter and surround with the grated ginger and scallions.

5 Pour the soy sauce into small, individual dipping bowls and serve individual portions of the wasabi.

6 To eat, mix wasabi to taste into the soy sauce and dip the mackerel pieces in the sauce before eating with the hot rice.

Mixed vegetables and rice
(Maze gohan)

Preparation and cooking:
1½ hours

Serves 4
3½ cups short-grain rice
1 large dried shiitake mushroom
2 carrots, sliced
1 inch piece of fresh gingerroot,
  pared and chopped
12 canned ginkgo nuts, drained
2 celery stalks, chopped
2 tablespoons soy sauce
1 tablespoon sake
½ teaspoon salt
4 cups water
⅔ cup frozen peas
⅔ cup shelled shrimp

1 Soak the rice following the directions for Plain boiled rice (see page 62).

2 Meanwhile, soak the mushroom in lukewarm water for 20 minutes, then drain and finely chop.

3 Drain the rice and put in a large, heavy-bottomed saucepan. Add the mushroom, carrots, ginger, ginkgo nuts, celery, soy sauce, sake and salt. Pour over the water and bring to a boil. Cover pan, reduce the heat to low and simmer the rice for 15-20 minutes, or until it is cooked and the water absorbed.

4 Stir in the peas and shrimp and simmer for a further 10 minutes. If the mixture becomes a little dry, add 1-2 tablespoons water. Transfer to a warmed serving dish and serve at once.

Mixed vegetables and rice (Maze gohan)

Three-colored rice
(Mi-iro gohan)

Preparation and cooking:
1 hour

Serves 4-6
2¼ cups short-grain rice
2½ cups water
1 package (7 oz) frozen peas
Meat
¾ lb ground top round of beef
3 tablespoons soy sauce
1 teaspoon salt
3 tablespoons sugar
⅔ cup dashi (Japanese stock), see
page 10
Eggs
5 eggs, lightly beaten
1 tablespoon sugar
1 tablespoon vegetable oil
¼ teaspoon salt

1 Soak and cook the rice following the directions given for Plain boiled rice (see page 62).

2 Meanwhile, prepare the meat. Combine all the meat ingredients in a small saucepan and cook over medium heat, stirring constantly, until the meat loses its pinkness and is broken up into small grains. Cook for a further 5 minutes, or until the meat is cooked though. Remove from the heat and keep hot.

3 Beat all the egg ingredients together and put into a small saucepan. Cook over low heat, stirring constantly, until the eggs scramble and become dry. Remove from the heat and keep hot.

4 Cook the peas in boiling salted water for 3-5 minutes. Remove from the heat, drain and set aside.

5 To assemble, fill individual serving bowls with rice. Level the top and arrange the meat mixture, egg mixture and peas decoratively on the top in 3 sections. Pour over any juices from the meat pan and serve at once.

Tempura with rice
(Tendon)

Preparation and cooking:
1 hour

Serves 4-6
2¼ cups short-grain rice
2½ cups water
Tempura
4-6 jumbo shrimp, body shells
removed and tails left on
3 small flounder fillets, quartered
1 sweet red pepper, seeded and
cut in squares
6 button mushrooms
vegetable oil for deep-frying
Batter
1 small egg, lightly beaten
⅓ cup water
½ cup flour
Sauce
¾ cup dashi (Japanese stock), see
page 10
3 tablespoons sake
3 tablespoons soy sauce
½ teaspoon sugar
½ inch piece of fresh gingerroot,
pared and grated
For garnish
2 scallions, chopped

1 Soak and cook the rice following the directions given for Plain boiled rice (see page 62).

2 Meanwhile, make the sauce. Put the dashi, sake, soy sauce and sugar into a saucepan and bring to a boil over low heat, stirring until the sugar has dissolved. Stir in the grated ginger and keep hot.

3 Prepare the tempura. Arrange the seafood and vegetables on a platter.

4 Fill a small, heavy-bottomed saucepan with oil to a depth of 3¼ inches and heat to 325°F.

5 Prepare the batter. Place the egg and water in a mixing bowl and mix lightly. Add the flour all at once and mix lightly with chopsticks — the batter will be lumpy. Dip the seafood and vegetable pieces in the batter and coat thoroughly.

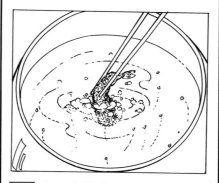

6 Carefully lower the pieces into the oil, a few at a time, and cook until they are crisp and golden brown. Using a slotted spoon or chopsticks, transfer the pieces to absorbent kitchen paper to drain.

7 To serve, transfer the rice to a warmed serving bowl and arrange the tempura pieces decoratively over the top. Pour over the sauce and garnish with all the chopped scallions.

Mushrooms and rice
(Shiitake gohan)

Preparation and cooking:
1 hour

Serves 4-6
2¼ cups rice
2½ cups water, plus 2 tablespoons
4 dried shiitake mushrooms
1 tablespoon vegetable oil
1 tablespoon soy sauce
½ teaspoon salt

1 Soak and cook the rice following the directions given for Plain boiled rice (see page 62).

2 Meanwhile, soak the mushrooms in lukewarm water for 20 minutes to soften. Drain, then trim off the stems and discard. Slice the trimmed mushrooms.

3 Heat the oil in a small saucepan, then add the mushrooms and sauté gently for 5 minutes. Add the soy sauce, salt and 2 tablespoons water and simmer gently, covered, for 5 minutes.

4 Remove the lid and continue to cook until the liquid has reduced and the mushrooms are only just moist.

5 Combine the hot, cooked rice and mushrooms, then cover and let stand for 5 minutes before serving.

Green rice
(Nameshi)

Preparation and cooking:
1 hour

Serves 4-6
2¼ cups rice
2½ cups water
½ lb fresh spinach, washed and drained
salt

1 Soak and cook the rice following the directions given for Plain boiled rice (see page 62).

2 Meanwhile, put the spinach in a small saucepan with only the water that clings to the leaves. Cover the pan and cook over medium heat for about 5 minutes until the spinach is soft and tender.

3 Rinse the spinach under cold running water, then drain well and gently press out as much moisture as possible.

4 Cut the spinach in shreds, add salt to taste and stir into the cooked rice. Serve at once.

● Green rice can also be made with watercress – use 1 large bunch instead of the spinach.

Tea and rice
(Ochazuke)

Preparation and cooking:
1¼ hours

Serves 4
2¼ cups short-grain rice
2½ cups water
4 sheets of nori seaweed
4 cups hot green tea

1 Soak and cook the rice following the directions given for Plain boiled rice (see page 62).

2 Preheat the broiler to medium high. Place the nori on the broiler rack and broil until it is crisp.

3 To serve, divide the rice among individual bowls and pour over the hot tea. Crumble a sheet of nori over each bowl and serve.

● This quick snack is a favorite Japanese method of using up leftover rice. Green tea is normally used, but you can substitute your own favorite brand or flavour, if wished.

Noodles

Japanese noodles, ranging from the wheat flour udon variety to the buckwheat soba type, are used imaginatively to create a variety of warming dishes.

Pepper and pork noodles
(Piman to butaniku-iri soba)

Preparation and cooking:
40 minutes

Serves 4
*6 oz soba noodles
salt
2 tablespoons vegetable oil
1 sweet red, 1 green and
1 yellow pepper, seeded
and cut into 2 x ¼ inch strips
½ lb lean pork, cut in
½ inch cubes
⅔ cup shelled shrimp
1 tablespoon sake
shichimi togarashi*

1 Cook the soba noodles. Bring a large pan of salted water to a boil. Add the soba noodles, bring back to a boil and cook for 7-10 minutes until tender but still firm to the bite.

2 Meanwhile, heat the oil in a skillet, add the peppers and cook for 3 minutes, stirring.

3 Add the pork cubes and cook, stirring, for a further 8 minutes.

4 Stir in the shrimp and sake and season to taste with shichimi togarashi. Cook for 2 minutes.

5 Drain the noodles, then rinse and arrange in 4 individual bowls. Spoon over the pork mixture and serve.

● Thinly sliced top round or rump steak can be used instead of pork. Or use cooked chicken and heat through with the shrimp. Spaghetti or tagliatelle can be substituted very successfully.

Pepper and pork noodles (Piman to butaniku-iri soba)

Soft fried udon
(Itame udon)

Preparation and cooking:
30 minutes

Serves 4
¾ lb udon noodles
salt
¼ cup vegetable oil
1 garlic clove, crushed
1 tablespoon grated fresh
gingerroot
½ carrot, peeled and grated
1½ cups shredded Chinese
cabbage
1 green pepper, seeded and diced
soy sauce
freshly ground black pepper

1 Bring a large saucepan of salted water to a boil. Add the noodles, bring back to a boil and cook for 7-10 minutes until just tender but still firm to the bite. Drain the noodles, then rinse under cold water and drain again.

2 Stir 1 tablespoon of the oil into the noodles and set aside. Heat the remaining oil in a large skillet, add the garlic and ginger and cook gently for 2-3 minutes.

3 Add the carrot, cabbage and green pepper to the pan and cook gently for 5 minutes until the vegetables are just softened.

4 Stir in the noodles and heat through gently, stirring constantly. Season to taste with soy sauce and black pepper and serve.

Casserole noodles with floating eggs
(Tsukimi udon)

Preparation and cooking:
30 minutes

Serves 4
¾ lb udon noodles
salt
5 cups water
2 tablespoons soy sauce
3 tablespoons mirin (sweet rice wine)
2 teaspoons sugar
¼ lb button mushrooms, washed
2 small leeks, cut in 2 inch lengths
4 eggs
For garnish
2 tablespoons minced fresh parsley
shichimi togarashi

1 Bring a large saucepan of salted water to a boil. Add the noodles, bring back to a boil and cook for 5 minutes until almost tender. Drain the noodles, then rinse under cold water and drain again.

2 Place the noodles in a Dutch oven and add the water, soy sauce, mirin and sugar.

3 Bring slowly to a boil, then add the mushrooms and leeks. Carefully break in 4 eggs so that they are well spaced.

4 Reduce the heat, cover the dish and simmer gently until the eggs are cooked.

5 Garnish the dish with parsley and shichimi togarashi and serve.

Deep-fried noodles
(Yaki soba)

Preparation and cooking:
45 minutes

Serves 4
½ lb soba noodles
salt
2½ tablespoons vegetable oil
1 garlic clove, crushed
2 teaspoons grated fresh gingerroot
1 onion, cut in eighths
1 green pepper, seeded and cut into ½ inch strips
1 cup sliced mushrooms
vegetable oil for deep-frying
2 teaspoons cornstarch, mixed to a paste with a little water
1 tablespoon soy sauce

1 Bring a large saucepan of salted water to a boil. Add the noodles, bring back to a boil and cook for 7-10 minutes until just tender but still firm to the bite. Drain the noodles, then rinse under cold water and drain again. Moisten with ½ tablespoon of the oil.

2 Heat the remaining oil in a saucepan, add the garlic and ginger and sauté gently for 1 minute.

3 Add the onion and green pepper and continue to fry over medium heat for 2-3 minutes. Stir in the sliced mushrooms and cook for 5 minutes until soft.

4 Add enough water to the pan to barely cover the vegetables. Bring to a boil, then simmer for 15 minutes.

5 Meanwhile, deep fry the noodles. Fill a heavy-bottomed saucepan with oil to a depth of 4 inches and heat to 350. Separate the noodles into strands and drop handfuls at a time into the hot oil. Fry until lightly browned.

6 Remove the fried noodles with a slotted spoon or chopsticks, drain on absorbent kitchen paper and keep warm while frying the remainder.

7 Add the cornstarch paste and soy sauce to the simmering vegetables and cook, stirring, until the mixture thickens.

8 To serve, divide the deep-fried noodles among 4 bowls, pour over the sauce and serve at once.

Noodles with pork
(Buta udon)

Preparation and cooking:
30 minutes

Serves 4-6
5 cups dashi (Japanese stock) see
page 10
10 oz lean pork, cut in thin strips
2 leeks, cut in 1 inch lengths
3 tablespoons soy sauce
1½ tablespoons sugar
salt
¾ lb udon noodles
For garnish
2 scallions, minced
2 carrots, cut in thin strips

1 Pour the dashi into a large saucepan and bring to a boil. Add the pork strips and leeks and cook for 5-8 minutes, or until the meat strips are cooked through.

2 Off heat, stir in the soy sauce and sugar. Keep hot.

3 Meanwhile, bring a large saucepan of salted water to a boil. Add the udon noodles, bring back to a boil and cook for 7-10 minutes, until just tender but still firm to the bite.

4 Drain the noodles and stir them into the soup. Increase the heat to medium and bring the soup to a boil.

5 To serve, divide the soup among 4-6 bowls and garnish with minced scallions and carrot strips. Serve at once.

Fox noodles
(Kitsune donburi)

Preparation and cooking:
1 hour

Serves 6
6 pieces of aburage (fried bean
curd), halved and parboiled
to remove excess oil
½ cup dashi (Japanese stock), see
page 10
⅓ cup soy sauce
2 tablespoons mirin (sweet rice
wine)
2 tablespoons sugar
Noodles
½ lb Udon noodles
salt
Kakejiru soup
5 cups dashi
½ cup soy sauce
½ cup mirin
½ teaspoon salt
2 scallions, thinly sliced

1 Put the aburage, dashi, soy sauce, mirin and sugar in a saucepan and bring to a boil. Reduce the heat to low and simmer for 20-25 minutes, or until the aburage has absorbed most of liquid.

2 Meanwhile, prepare the noodles. Bring a large saucepan of salted water to a boil. Add the udon noodles, bring back to a boil and cook for 7-10 minutes until just tender but still firm to the bite. Drain the noodles, then rinse and drain again. Return to the saucepan. Keep hot.

3 Make the soup. Put the dashi, soy sauce, mirin, salt and scallions into a second large saucepan. Bring to a boil, reduce the heat to low and simmer the soup for about 10 minutes.

4 Divide noodles among 6 individual soup bowls. Place 2 pieces of aburage on top of each portion. Pour over the soup, then serve at once.

● The unusual name of this dish comes about because, according to folklore, the fox is very partial to bean curd which, together with udon noodles, is the main ingredient of this dish.

Overleaf: Left, Fox noodles (Kitsune donburi). Right, Noodles with pork (Buta udon).

Deep-fried food coated in harusame noodles
(Tempura harusame)

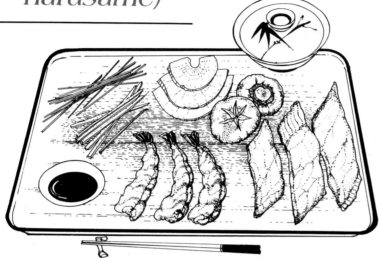

Preparation and cooking:
1 hour

Serves 8
8 jumbo shrimp, shelled
1 cod fillet, skinned and cut in
2 inch pieces
1 large flounder fillet, skinned and
cut in 2 inch pieces
8 button mushrooms
2 sea scallops, quartered
1 canned bamboo shoot, drained
and cut in 2 inch pieces
1 carrot, sliced
½ cup flour
2 egg whites, beaten
6 oz harusame noodles, cut in
small pieces
vegetable oil for deep-frying
Dipping sauce
¾ cup dashi (Japanese stock), see
page 10
2 tablespoons soy sauce
2 tablespoons mirin (sweet rice
wine)
1 teaspoon grated daikon
(Japanese white radish)

1 Arrange the shrimp, cod, flounder, button mushrooms, scallops, bamboo shoot and carrot on a large platter.

2 Place the flour, egg whites and harusame noodles in separate dishes. Dip the food, 1 piece at a time, first in the flour, shaking off any excess, then in the egg whites and finally roll in the harusame noodles until evenly coated. Set aside.

3 Fill a cast-iron sukiyaki pan (sukiyaki-nabe) or deep, heavy-bottomed skillet about one-third full with vegetable oil and heat until very hot.

4 Carefully lower the food pieces, 2 or 3 at a time, into the oil and fry until they are golden brown and the noodles have expanded. Remove from the oil and drain on absorbent kitchen paper. Keep hot while cooking the remaining pieces in the same way.

5 Make dipping sauce. Put dashi, soy sauce and mirin into a saucepan. Bring to a boil, then stir in the grated daikon. Remove from the heat and pour into dipping bowls.

6 Serve the food piping hot, with the dipping sauce.

● Harusame are small white noodles similar in texture to Chinese cellophane noodles and these can be used if harusame noodles are difficult to obtain.
● Harusame expand in the oil while frying and provide a deliciously crunchy coating for the succulent fish and vegetables.

Noodles with cabbage
(Kyabetsu-iri udon)

Preparation and cooking:
25 minutes

Serves 4
¼ lb udon noodles
salt
2 tablespoons vegetable oil
6 scallions, sliced
1 tablespoon grated fresh root
ginger
1 lb Chinese cabbage, cut in
½ inch thick slices
1 cup chopped lean
cooked ham
2 cups beansprouts
1 tablespoon soy sauce
¼ cup chicken stock
freshly ground black pepper

1 Bring a large saucepan of salted water to a boil. Add the udon noodles, bring back to a boil and cook for 7-10 minutes until just tender but still firm to the bite. Drain and rinse then set aside.

2 Heat the oil in a large skillet, add the onions and ginger and sauté gently for 2 minutes, stirring constantly.

3 Add the cabbage to the pan with the chopped ham. Cook gently for a further 2 minutes, stirring mixture constantly.

4 Add the drained udon noodles, together with the beansprouts, soy sauce, stock and salt and pepper to taste. Increase the heat to medium and stir-fry for about 5 minutes until the vegetables are tender but still crisp and most of the liquid in the pan has evaporated.

5 To serve, spoon into a warmed serving dish or 4 individual bowls.

Ice noodles
(Hiyashi somen)

Preparation and cooking:
1¼ hours

Serves 6
1 lb somen noodles
salt
2 hard-cooked eggs, thinly sliced
2 tomatoes, thinly sliced
⅓ cucumber, pared and cubed
¾ cup cubed lean cooked ham
4 mint leaves, cut in strips
Sauce
2 dried shiitake mushrooms
4 cups dashi (Japanese stock), see
page 10
⅔ cup soy sauce
2 tablespoons sugar
⅔ cup sake

1 Soak the mushrooms for the sauce in lukewarm water for 20 minutes to soften. Drain, then trim the stems and chop the mushrooms.

2 Meanwhile, bring a large saucepan of salted water to a boil. Add the somen noodles, bring back to a boil and cook for 5 minutes until just tender but still firm to the bite.

3 Drain and rinse the noodles under cold running water. Transfer to a bowl and put into the refrigerator for 30 minutes.

4 While the noodles are chilling, make the sauce. Put the dashi into a large saucepan and add all the remaining sauce ingredients. Bring to a boil; boil briskly for 8 minutes. Remove from the heat and let cool.

5 Arrange the eggs, tomatoes, cucumber and ham decoratively on a large serving platter and sprinkle over the mint strips.

6 To serve, put the somen noodles on a bed of ice cubes, or sprinkle them with ice chips. Pour the sauce mixture into 6 individual serving bowls. Each guest helps him or herself to a portion of each dish, dipping the noodles into the sauce before eating.

One-pot

The idea of a one-pot dish is that it can be cooked at the table, over a hot ring – the cooking becomes part of the enjoyment of the meal. Ingredients are arranged artistically on a serving platter and guests dip their own portion into a pot of bubbling oil or broth. A marvellous dish for a party!

Beef Sukiyaki 1

Preparation and cooking:
1¾ hours

Serves 4
1¼ lb fillet steak, thinly
sliced across the grain
1 onion, sliced into very thin rings
3 green onions, cut in 1 inch
lengths
½ cup sliced mushrooms, sliced
6 oz fresh spinach, washed, dried,
trimmed and cut in strips
2 firm tomatoes, blanched,
peeled, seeded and diced
1 small bunch of watercress,
washed and trimmed
1 can (8 oz) bamboo shoots,
drained and thinly sliced
1 cup tofu (bean curd), cut in 4
(1½ x ½ inch) cubes
¼ cup corn oil
Teriyaki sauce
¼ cup soy sauce
⅓ cup mirin (sweet rice wine)
2 tablespoons sugar
Sansho sauce
2 scallions, thinly sliced
⅓ cup soy sauce
⅓ cup sake
2 tablespoons soft light brown
sugar
¼ teaspoon ground sansho
(Japanese pepper)
Japanese ginger sauce
2 teaspoons soy sauce
½ chicken bouillon cube
2 tablespoons mirin
¼ cup water
1 teaspoon soft brown sugar
2 teaspoons grated fresh
gingerroot
4 teaspoons minced scallion
Cooking sauce
¼ cup sake
1 tablespoon soft light brown
sugar
1 tablespoon corn oil
⅓ cup soy sauce
To serve
4 eggs
2¼ cups short-grain rice, cooked

1 Cut the thin beef slices into 1½ inch squares.

2 Arrange the cut raw meat and the prepared vegetables and tofu decoratively on a large platter or wooden board.

3 Make the teriyaki sauce. Place all the sauce ingredients in a small saucepan and simmer over low heat, stirring constantly with a wooden spoon, until the sauce begins to thicken slightly. Remove from the heat and let cool.

4 Make the sansho sauce. Place all the sauce ingredients in a small saucepan and simmer over low heat, stirring constantly with a wooden spoon, until the sauce begins to thicken. Let cool.

5 Make the Japanese ginger sauce. Place all the sauce ingredients in a small saucepan and simmer over low heat until the sugar has dissolved, stirring occasionally. Let cool.

6 For each guest, set 4 dipping bowls. Break an egg into 1 of the bowls and beat lightly. Put a portion of each of the serving sauces in the other 3 bowls.

7 In a small bowl, mix the ingredients for the cooking sauce.

8 Heat 1 tablespoon corn oil in a cast-iron sukiyaki pan (sukiyaki-nabe) or a deep, heavy-bottomed skillet. Add enough cooking sauce to cover the base of the hot pan.

9 Place 1 portion of the meat pieces in the sauce and cook for 1 minute. Add a portion of the vegetables and tofu and continue to cook for 1 minute.

10 After 1 minute, turn the mixture, so that the vegetables are at the bottom and the meat pieces on top. Add a little more sauce, if necessary, and continue cooking for 3 minutes over medium heat, until the vegetables are tender but still crisp.

11 Serve the food as soon as it is cooked, then repeat the process with the remaining food. The liquid should always be simmering. If the food begins to stick, add 1 teaspoon cold water to cool it.

12 The cooked food should be dipped first into the egg, then into one of the sauces before eating.

● Dipping the hot food into raw egg yolk helps to cool the food.

Beef sukiyaki 2

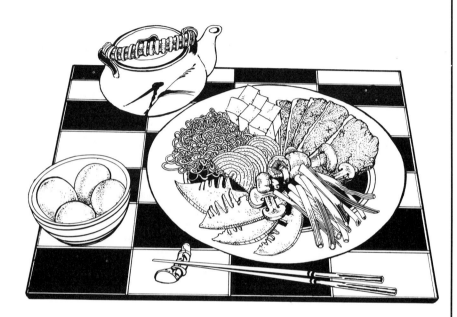

Preparation and cooking:
45 minutes

Serves 4
10 scallions
9 oz shirataki noodles, drained
and rinsed
1 lb fillet steak, thinly sliced
across the grain
1 onion, cut in thin wedges
2 cups tofu (bean curd), cut in
1 inch cubes
¼ lb shungiku (Japanese
chrysanthemum leaves)
1 cup sliced canned bamboo
shoots
8 button mushrooms, thinly sliced
1 tablespoon vegetable oil
4 eggs
Cooking sauce
½ cup soy sauce
½ cup mirin (sweet rice wine)
½ cup dashi (Japanese stock), see
page 10
1 tablespoon sugar

1 Trim the scallions, to leave 3 inches of the green part attached to the bulbs, then slice in 2 inch diagonal slices.

2 Cook the noodles in boiling water for 1 minute, then drain and cut in half.

3 Arrange the beef slices, scallions, onion, tofu cubes, shungiku, bamboo shoots, sliced mushrooms and drained shirataki noodles on a large platter or wooden board.

4 Make the cooking sauce. Combine the soy sauce, mirin, dashi and sugar in a small saucepan. Bring to a boil, then pour into a small pitcher or bowl.

5 Break each of the eggs into a separate small bowl and set aside.

6 Heat the vegetable oil in a cast-iron sukiyaki pan (sukiyaki-nabe) or a deep, heavy-bottomed skillet. Add half the beef and cook for 1-2 minutes without turning. Add the scallions and onion, then pour half of the cooking sauce over the pan ingredients. Add half the shirataki noodles, tofu, shungiku, bamboo shoots and mushrooms and cook stirring with chop-sticks for 3-4 minutes.

7 Serve the food as soon as it is cooked, then cook the remaining ingredients in the same way.

8 The cooked food should be dipped into the egg before eating.

● When all the food has been eaten, plain boiled rice may be added to the remaining pan juices and lightly heated through.

Fish and vegetable casserole
(Chiri nabe)

Preparation and cooking:
45 minutes

Serves 4-6
1 small Chinese cabbage head trimmed
1 large pompano or other firm white fish, cleaned and filleted
2 cups sliced mushrooms
1 carrot, cut into 1 inch lengths
3 leeks, cut in ½ inch lengths
2 cups tofu (bean curd), cubed
5 cups dashi (Japanese stock) see page 10
Dipping sauce
⅔ cup soy sauce
6 scallions, chopped
1 small turnip, grated
juice of 2 lemons

1 Bring a large saucepan of water to a boil, add the whole cabbage and cook for 5 minutes. Drain, then chop diagonally in 2 inch lengths.

2 Cut the fish in large pieces and arrange the fish, cabbage, mushrooms, carrot, leeks and tofu on a large serving platter.

3 Make the dipping sauce. Mix the soy sauce, scallions, turnip and lemon juice together and divide between 4-6 individual dipping bowls.

4 Pour the dashi into a Dutch oven or pot and bring to a boil. Add the food to the dashi, a few pieces at a time, and cook for 3-5 minutes, or until they are cooked through. Replenish the pot as necessary.

5 The cooked food should be dipped into the sauce before eating.

Beef with cabbage and spinach
(Shabu shabu)

Preparation and cooking:
50 minutes

Serves 4
1 white cabbage, separated into leaves
12 button mushrooms
4 cups chopped fresh spinnach, washed
1 cup tofu (bean curd), cubed
1½ lb rump steak, thinly sliced across the grain
5 cups dashi (Japanese stock), see page 10
Sauce
⅔ cup soy sauce
1-2 tablespoons grated daikon (Japanese white radish) or icicle radish
4 scallions, minced
juice of 2 lemons

1 Cook the cabbage leaves gently for 3 minutes, then drain and remove from the saucepan. Roll up the leaves into neat rolls.

2 Arrange all the vegetables and tofu decoratively on a serving platter. Arrange the beef slices on a second platter. Set aside.

3 Make the sauce. Mix the soy sauce, grated daikon, scallions and lemon juice together and pour into 4 individual dipping bowls.

4 Pour the dashi into a Dutch oven or pot and bring to a boil. Cook the food in the dashi, a few pieces at a time, until just tender.

5 The cooked food should be dipped into the sauce before eating.

● The Japanese name of this dish comes from the sound the ingredients make as they are being cooked in the dashi.

Overleaf: Beef sukiyaki 2

Chicken and oyster casserole
(Yosenabe)

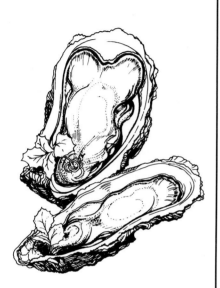

Preparation and cooking:
1 hour

Serves 6

4 cups dashi (Japanese stock), see
page 10
2 chicken breasts, skinned, boned
and cubed
2 large carrots, sliced
1⅓ cups thinly sliced daikon
(Japanese white radish)
¼ cup soy sauce
⅔ cup sake
½ lb shirataki noodles, drained
and rinsed
3 sheets of nori seaweed, cubed
6 scallions, cut in short lengths
12 uncooked shrimp, shelled
12 shucked oysters or clams
½ lb cod fillet, skinned and cubed
18 button mushrooms, stems
removed

1 Pour the dashi into a large saucepan and bring to a boil. Reduce the heat to low, add the chicken cubes and simmer for 10 minutes, or until the cubes are almost tender.

2 Add the carrots and daikon and simmer for a further 5 minutes. Remove the pan from the heat and transfer the chicken and vegetables to a plate. Strain the stock into a Dutch oven or pot and stir in the soy sauce and sake. Bring to a boil.

3 Arrange all the remaining ingredients on a large serving platter.

4 Cook the ingredients in the hot stock for 1-2 minutes before eating. When all the ingredients have been cooked, the stock may be served as a soup.

● Yosenabe literally means a "collection of everything" so the ingredients here are just suggestions and can be changed for almost anything suitable.

Pork and vegetables in stock
(Botan nabe)

Preparation and cooking:
50 minutes

Serves 6

1 lb carrots, cut in ¼ inch lengths
1 white cabbage, separated into
leaves
½ lb mushrooms
1½ lb lean pork, very thinly sliced
3 garlic cloves, crushed
1½ inch piece of fresh gingerroot,
pared and chopped
1 cup soy sauce
6 scallions, minced
2 lemons, cut in small wedges
2 cups dashi (Japanese stock), see
page 10

1 Lightly cook the carrots and cabbage separately in boiling water for 3 minutes.

2 Drain and roll up the cabbage leaves, then arrange the carrots, cabbage rolls and mushrooms decoratively on a serving platter.

3 Arrange the pork slices carefully in the shape of a flower on a serving plate and use the garlic and ginger to make the center of the flower.

4 Combine the soy sauce with about one fourth of the scallions and pour into 6 individual dipping bowls. Arrange the lemon wedges and remaining scallions in separate serving bowls.

5 Pour the dashi into a Dutch oven or pot and bring to a boil. Add a few pieces of the pork and cook until it is white. Cook a portion of the other ingredients in the same way. Replenish the pot as necessary.

6 The cooked food should be dipped into the sauce before eating. When all the ingredients have been cooked, the stock may be served as a soup.

● This dish gets its name from the Japanese word for peony because the pork slices are arranged in the shape of a peony before cooking.

Fish sukiyaki

Preparation and cooking:
2 hours

Serves 4-6
4 cups dashi (Japanese stock), see
page 10
1 tablespoon sugar
1/4 cup sake
salt
9 large Chinese cabbage leaves
1/2 lb fresh spinach
1 lb fish fillets (cod, whiting,
salmon or mackerel), thinly sliced
6 scallions, cut in 1 1/2 inch lengths
2 bamboo shoots, thinly sliced
2 cups tofu (bean curd), cut into 1
inch cubes
2 tablespoons vegetable oil
Dipping sauce
2 inch piece of fresh gingerroot,
pared and grated
juice of 1 lemon
1/4 cup soy sauce

1 Combine the dashi, sugar and sake in a bowl.

2 Bring a pan of salted water to a boil and lightly boil the Chinese leaves for about 30 seconds. Lift them from the pot and reserve the water. Rinse the leaves under cold water and drain.

3 Gather the spinach leaves together in a bunch, with the stems all at one end. Return the salted water to the boil and, holding a small bunch of spinach by the stems, dip into the water for about 30 seconds. Rinse under cold water and drain. Repeat this process with the remaining spinach.

4 Arrange 3 Chinese leaves with stems and leaves alternately overlapping on a bamboo mat (sudare) or heavy moist cloth. Lay a third of the spinach leaves horizontally across the centre, alternating leaves and stems. Roll the cabbage leaves and spinach leaves into a tight bundle. Remove the bamboo mat or cloth, and cut into 1 inch lengths. Repeat this process with the remaining cabbage and spinach.

5 Make the sauce. Combine the ginger, lemon juice and soy sauce and place in a small serving bowl.

6 Arrange the cabbage rolls together with the fish, scallions, bamboo shoots and tofu on a serving platter.

7 Heat the oil in a cast-iron sukiyaki pan (sukiyaki-nabe) or a deep, heavy-bottomed skillet.

8 Add the fish and lightly cook on both sides, then add half the prepared vegetables and tofu. Pour in two-thirds of the dashi mixture and cook until the vegetables are tender.

9 Replenish the pan with the remaining vegetables, tofu and dashi as required.

10 The cooked food should be dipped into the sauce before eating.

Overleaf: Chicken with vegetables
(Toriniku mizutaki)

Tokyo Hotchpot
(Oden)

豆腐

Preparation and cooking:
3½ hours

Serves 8
10 cups dashi (Japanese stock),
see page 10
⅓ cup soy sauce
1½ tablespoons sugar
1 large squid, cleaned and cut
in rings
2 turnips, cut in chunks
2 large carrots, cut in flowers
4 potatoes, cut in chunks
2 cakes of konnyaku (gelatinous
white cakes), cut in triangles
4 pieces of aburage, (fried bean
curd), cut in triangles and par-
cooked to remove excess oil
4 hard-cooked eggs
1 cup tofu (bean curd), cubed
Meatballs
¾ lb ground beef
2 scallions, minced
1 inch piece of fresh gingerroot,
pared and grated
1½ tablespoons flour
2 teaspoons soy sauce
2 small eggs, beaten
vegetable oil for deep-frying
To serve
wasabi (Japanese horseradish
mustard), mixed to a
paste with water

1 First prepare the meat-balls. Combine the beef, scallions, ginger, flour, soy sauce and eggs in a large bowl. Using the palms of your hands, gently shape the mixture into small balls, about 1 inch in diameter.

2 Fill a large, deep skillet about one-third with oil and heat until very hot.

3 Carefully lower the meat-balls, a few at a time, into the oil and cook until they are golden brown. Using a slotted spoon, remove the meatballs from the oil and drain on absorbent kitchen paper. Keep hot while cooking the remaining meatballs in the same way. Set aside.

4 Pour the dashi into a deep, heavy-bottomed saucepan and add the soy sauce and sugar, stir well, then add the remaining ingredients, including the meatballs but excepting the tofu, to the pan and bring to a boil.

5 Reduce the heat to very low and simmer for 2-3 hours. Add the tofu about 30 minutes before you wish to serve the dish. Serve with wasabi to taste.

● Street stalls selling this warming dish — which is supposed to have originated in Tokyo — are a common sight during winter in Japan. It is also a good dish for parties as it can be left on a very low heat until needed.

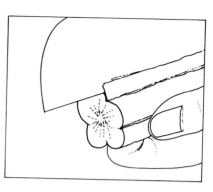

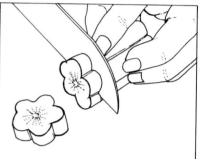

● To make carrot flowers, cut a piece of carrot, 3 inches long. Make 5 slits, lengthwise, around the carrot piece, then slice away at each slit to make round petal shapes.
Cut the shaped carrot pieces in slices, then smooth off the edges of each slice.

Beef with vegetables
(Gyuniku mizutaki)

Preparation and cooking:
1 hour

Serves 4
1 lb fillet steak, very thinly sliced
2 cups sliced mushrooms
1 small cauliflower, cut in
flowerets
3 cups roughly chopped Chinese
cabbage
2 green peppers, seeded and cut
in ½ inch wide strips
6 scallions, cut in 1½ inch
lengths
2 cups tofu (bean curd), cut in 1
inch cubes
9 cups dashi (Japanese stock), see
page 10
4 eggs
Sesame sauce
1 cup sesame seeds, toasted
1 cup dashi (Japanese stock), see
page 10
½ teaspoon hot pepper sauce

1 Arrange the sliced beef, mushrooms, cauliflower, cabbage, green peppers, scallions and tofu decoratively on 1 or 2 serving dishes.

2 Make the sesame sauce. Combine all the ingredients and divide among 4 small dipping bowls.

3 Pour the dashi into a Dutch oven or pot and bring to a boil. Cook the food in the dashi a few pieces at a time, until they are just cooked. The cooked food should be dipped into the sauce before eating.

4 Toward the end of the meal, break the eggs into the simmering broth and poach. Using a slotted spoon, transfer the poached eggs to guests' individual bowls and ladle the remaining dashi over the eggs.

Chicken with vegetables
(Toriniku mizutaki)

Preparation and cooking:
1 hour

Serves 4
4 chicken breasts, skinned, boned
and cut in bite-size pieces
1 cup tofu (bean curd), cubed
½ lb mushrooms, stems removed
1 small Chinese cabbage head
1 bunch of watercress
4 carrots, thinly sliced
2 leeks, cut diagonally in 1 inch
lengths
2 cups dashi (Japanese stock), see
page 10
Dipping sauce
¾ cup soy sauce
lemon slices
grated daikon (Japanese white
radish)

1 Arrange the chicken and tofu on a serving platter. Slice the mushroom caps and chop the Chinese leaves and watercress. Arrange all the vegetables on a serving platter.

2 Make the dipping sauce. Divide the soy sauce among individual dipping bowls and garnish with lemon slices and grated radish.

3 Pour the dashi into a deep, Dutch oven or pot and bring to a boil. Reduce the heat to low and add some chicken and vegetables. Cook for 3-5 minutes, or until the meat is just cooked through. Replenish the pot when it is necessary.

4 The cooked food should be dipped into the sauce before eating.

Vegetables

The Japanese repertoire of vegetable dishes ranges from exotic pickles to unusual hot salads. To achieve an authentic touch, the vegetables must be of the highest quality and the utmost care must be taken in the preparation.

Vegetable tempura

Preparation and cooking:
1¼ hours

Serves 4
½ eggplant, halved lengthwise
salt
1 carrot, cut in 16 (⅛ inch thick) slices
4 green beans, cut 2 inch lengths
8 mushrooms, quartered
½ Bermuda onion, cut into ¼ inch slices and separated into rings
8 snow peas, trimmed
4 asparagus tips
vegetable oil for deep-frying
Dipping Sauce
1¼ cups dashi (Japanese stock), see page 10
¼ cup soy sauce
¼ cup sake
½ teaspoon sugar
pinch of ground ginger

Daikon dressing
1 daikon (Japanese white radish), finely grated
1 inch piece of fresh gingerroot, pared and finely grated
grated
Soy batter
1 egg
1 tablespoon soy sauce
1 cup water
1 cup flour

1 Slice the eggplant half lengthwise in 4 slices, discarding the end. Cut each slice in fourths. Put the pieces into a colander and sprinkle with salt. Let to drain for 30 minutes. Rinse the slices under cold water and dry well with absorbent kitchen paper.

2 Arrange the prepared vegetables on a serving platter.

Vegetable tempura

3 Make the dipping sauce. Pour the dashi into a small saucepan, add the remaining ingredients and bring to a boil over medium heat. Reduce the heat and simmer for 5 minutes, then remove from the heat. Divide the sauce among 4 bowls and put 1 bowl before each guest.

4 Make the daikon dressing. Mix the grated daikon and ginger together. Divide the mixture among 4 small bowls and place 1 before each guest.

5 Make the batter. Place the beaten egg, soy sauce and water in a medium-size bowl and beat lightly. Add the flour all at once and mix lightly with chopsticks – it will be lumpy in consistency

6 Fill a deep, heavy-bottomed saucepan with oil to a depth of 3¼ inches and heat to 350°F. Quickly dip a portion of vegetables in the batter and cook for about 1 minute until puffed and golden.

7 Remove the cooked vegetables from the oil and drain on a rack or on absorbent kitchen paper. Arrange the vegetables in groups on a warmed individual serving plate and serve immediately while you continue to cook all the remaining portions.

8 Each guest eats his or her portion as it is served, dipping the food in the sauce and dressing.

Vegetables in white sesame sauce
(*Shirasu ae*)

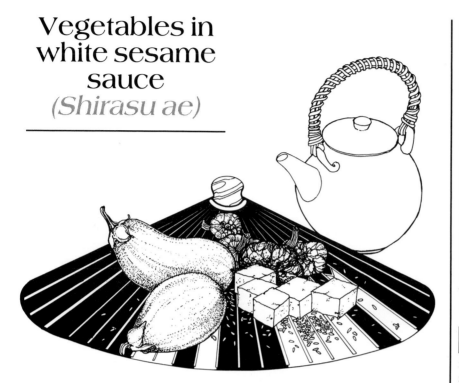

Preparation and cooking:
soaking, then 2 hours

Serves 6
1 cup dried white lima beans
soaked overnight
2 eggplants
salt
4 dried shiitake mushrooms
⅓ cup water
2 tablespoons soy sauce
2 teaspoons sugar
Sesame sauce
½ cup tofu (bean curd)
4 tablespoons white sesame seeds
1 tablespoon sugar
3 tablespoons vinegar
1 tablespoon mirin (sweet rice
wine)
½ teaspoon salt

1 Prepare the vegetables. Rinse the beans, put into a saucepan and cover with fresh water. Bring to a boil and boil briskly for 15 minutes, then reduce the heat and cook for 1 hour, or until tender.

2 Cook the eggplants in boiling salted water for 30 minutes or until tender. Drain and transfer to a chopping board. Cut the eggplants lengthwise in thin slices, then halve each round to make a half-moon shape. Set aside.

3 Soak the mushrooms in lukewarm water for 20 minutes to soften. Drain, then discard the stems and slice the mushrooms thinly.

4 Meanwhile, prepare the sauce. Bring a small saucepan of water to a boil, add the tofu, bring back to a boil and cook for 3 minutes. Drain well, then put the tofu into a cloth and gently squeeze out as much water as possible (the tofu should break up). Set aside.

5 Gently sauté the sesame seeds in a small skillet until they begin to "jump", taking care not to burn them. Remove from the heat and put them into a mortar. Grind with a pestle until the seeds form a paste (this may take some time – so be prepared!)

6 Stir the tofu into the mortar and continue to pound with the pestle for a further 3 minutes. Stir in the remaining sauce ingredients and continue pounding until the sauce is smooth and sticky and makes a sort of suction noise when the pestle is moved around the mortar. Set aside.

7 Put the water, soy sauce and sugar into a small saucepan and bring to a boil, stirring constantly until the sugar dissolves. Add the mushroom slices to the pan, reduce the heat to low and simmer for 10 minutes, so that the mushrooms absorb the flavor of the liquid. Drain the mushrooms and put into a cloth. Gently squeeze as much liquid as possible out of the mushrooms.

8 To serve, combine all the vegetables together, then pour over the sesame sauce. Stir gently to coat vegetables in the sauce and serve the dish at room temperature.

● This dish originated with Zen monks in Japan and is considered an exercise in skill to prepare – but although it is a little time-consuming, the result is well worth the effort. The "secret" of making a good *Shirasu ae* is to remove as much water from the vegetables as possible.

Fried eggplant in miso sauce
(Age nasu to miso dare)

Preparation and cooking:
30 minutes

Serves 6
1½ lb eggplants
2 teaspoons salt
2 tablespoons vegetable oil
2 tablespoons sesame oil
2-4 tablespoons miso (bean paste)
4-5 tablespoons water
3 tablespoons sake
1 tablespoon sugar
2 tablespoons lemon juice
For garnish
tomato wedges

1 Cut the eggplants into ¼ inch slices and cut each slice in strips. Sprinkle with salt and leave to drain for 5 minutes. Rinse under cold running water and dry on absorbent kitchen paper, or in a clean dish towel.

2 Heat both the oils in a large skillet. Add the eggplants and cook for 3 minutes, stirring, until the eggplants soften a little.

3 Dilute the miso paste with 4 tablespoons water, and add the sake and sugar. Add the miso mixture to the eggplants, mix well and simmer over a low heat for 3-4 minutes or until the eggplants are soft.

4 If the sauce begins to dry up, add a little more water. Add the lemon juice and transfer to a serving dish. Garnish with tomato wedges and serve at once.

Broiled leeks
(Negi shigi-yaki)

Preparation and cooking:
20 minutes

Serves 4
4 leeks, sliced in 1½ inch lengths
2 tablespoons vegetable oil
Sauce
1 tablespoon miso (bean paste)
1 tablespoon sugar
1 tablespoon mirin (sweet rice wine)

1 Preheat the broiler to medium high.

2 Thread the lengths of leeks onto 4 skewers, then brush liberally with the oil.

3 Combine the miso, sugar and mirin in a small bowl and set aside.

4 Broil the oiled leeks, turning frequently until they are lightly browned. Remove from the broiler and brush all over with the sauce.

5 Return the leeks to the broiler rack and broil again for about 2 minutes, turning frequently to avoid over-browning.

6 Transfer to a warmed serving dish and serve at once.

● Zucchini, sweet red or green peppers, eggplants or mushrooms may also be cooked in this way to make a delicious side dish.

Boiled spinach
(Horenso no ohitashi)

preparation and cooking:
20 minutes

Serves 4
1 lb fresh spinach
1 tablespoon katsuobushi (dried bonito flakes)
1 tablespoon soy sauce

1 Wash the spinach well, discarding any tough stems. Place in a saucepan with just the water that adheres to the leaves. Cook gently for 6-8 minutes, or until the spinach is tender, taking care not to overcook.

2 Drain the spinach, then arrange on a chopping board so that all the stems are facing the same way. Shred the spinach, in 1 inch sections. Then, section by section, gently squeeze out the water from the spinach.

3 Arrange the dry spinach on a serving plate and sprinkle over the katsuobushi and soy sauce. Serve cold.

● Watercress or romaine lettuce can also be cooked in this way.

Overleaf: Foreground, Vegetable kabobs (Yasai no kushiage). Back left, Green beans with sesame dressing (Ingen no goma joyu ae). Back right, Orange and white vinegared salad (Namasu).

Vegetable kabobs
(Yasai no kushiage)

Preparation and cooking:
45 minutes

Serves 4
3 eggs, lightly beaten
¾ cup dried bread crumbs
½ cup flour
½ cauliflower, separated into small flowerets
¼ lb mushrooms, stems removed
2 zucchini, sliced
2 onions, cut in eighths
vegetable oil for deep-frying
Sauce
1 tablespoon miso (bean paste)
1 teaspoon vinegar
⅔ cup mayonnaise

1 Make the sauce. Beat the miso and vinegar together until they are well blended, then stir into the mayonnaise. Set aside while cooking the vegetables.

2 Put the beaten eggs, bread crumbs and flour into separate, shallow bowls. Dip all the vegetable pieces first in the egg, then in the flour and finally in the bread crumbs, to coat well.

3 Thread the coated pieces onto metal skewers. (The skewers will be put into a large pan, so make sure the vegetables are arranged in such a way that they can be easily deep-fried.)

4 Fill a cast-iron sukiyaki pan (sukiyaki-nabe) or deep, heavy-bottomed skillet about one-third full with oil and heat it until it is very hot. Carefully lower the skewers into the hot oil and cook until the vegetables are deep golden. Remove the skewers from the oil and drain on absorbent kitchen paper.

5 Arrange the vegetable kabobs on serving platters and either pour over the sauce or serve it as an accompaniment. Serve at once.

Vegetable egg noodles
(Ramen)

Preparation and cooking:
soaking, then 2½ hours

Serves 4
1 tablespoon vegetable oil
2 garlic cloves, crushed
2 scallions, chopped
2 cups beansprouts
2 tablespoons soy sauce
¼ teaspoon shichimi togarashi
½ lb egg noodles
Vegetable stock
5 cups water
½ cup soy beans, soaked overnight and drained
⅔ cup chopped turnips
1 onion, chopped
1½ cups chopped cabbage
soy sauce
salt and freshly ground black pepper

1 Make the vegetable stock. Pour the water into a large saucepan and add the soy beans, turnips, onion and white cabbage. Bring to a boil, then reduce the heat and simmer gently for about 2 hours.

2 Strain the stock and season to taste with soy sauce, salt and black pepper. Set aside.

3 Heat the oil in a large saucepan, add the garlic and sauté gently until lightly golden. Add the scallions and beansprouts and stir-fry for a further 2 minutes.

4 Add the vegetable stock and soy sauce and bring to a boil. Stir in the shichimi togarashi, reduce the heat and then continue to simmer for 15 minutes.

5 Meanwhile, cook the noodles. Bring a large saucepan of salted water to a boil. Add the noodles, bring back to a boil and cook for 3-5 minutes until just tender but still firm to the bite. Drain.

6 Divide the noodles among 4 soup bowls and pour over the hot soup. Serve at once.

● The stock can be made up to 2 days in advance and stored in the refrigerator. It may be used as a substitute for dashi (see page 10) in soup recipes.

Green beans with sesame dressing
(Ingen no goma joyu ae)

Preparation and cooking:
30 minutes

Serves 4
2 cups chopped green beans
salt
Dressing
4 tablespoons white sesame seeds
2 tablespoons soy sauce
1 tablespoon sugar

1 Cook the beans in lightly salted boiling water for about 5 minutes or until they are just tender. Drain, then rinse in cold water. Dry on absorbent kitchen paper and set aside.

2 Sauté the sesame seeds gently in a small skillet until they begin to "jump", then pound in a mortar with a pestle to release the oil – this takes some time. When they form a reasonably smooth paste, stir in the soy sauce and sugar.

3 Arrange the beans in a serving dish and spoon over the dressing. Mix gently, making sure the beans are well coated. Serve at once.

Vegetables simmered in soy sauce
(Umani)

Preparation and cooking:
40 minutes

Serves 4-6
6 dried shiitake mushrooms
2 carrots, sliced diagonally in short lengths
1 can 8 oz canned bamboo shoots, drained and cut in 2 inch lengths
1 can (8 oz) konnyaku (gelatinous white cakes), drained and cut in 2 inch cubes
2½ cups dashi (Japanese stock), see page 10
⅓ cup soy sauce
2 tablespoons sugar
1 tablespoon mirin (sweet rice wine)
1 teaspoon salt
⅔ cup chopped green beans,
For garnish
2 inch piece of daikon (Japanese white radish), pared and cut in fine shreds

1 Soak the dried shiitake mushrooms in lukewarm water for 20 minutes to soften. Drain, then discard the stems.

2 Put the carrots, bamboo shoots and konnyaku into a saucepan and add the dashi, soy sauce, sugar, mirin and salt.

3 Bring to a boil, then reduce the heat and simmer for 15 minutes. Add the mushroom caps and green beans to the pan and simmer for a further 10 minutes.

4 Transfer to a warmed serving dish, garnish with daikon shreds and serve.

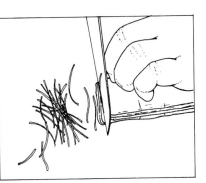

● To make very fine shreds of daikon for the garnish, use the "needle cut"' method – using a small sharp knife, cut the piece of daikon in thin slices, then cut the slices in fine shreds.

Overleaf: Omelet stuffed with spinach (Horenso tamago-yaki) and variation.

Omelet stuffed with spinach
(*Horenso tamago-yaki*)

Preparation and cooking:
25 minutes

Serves 4
10 oz fresh spinach
9 cups water
1 teaspoon sugar
2 teaspoons soy sauce
2 eggs
¼ teaspoon salt
vegetable oil for frying
For garnish
1 radish, cut in a waterlily shape
1 long slice of carrot, cut in a feather shape
1 tomato skin rose
thin strips of cucumber peel

1 Wash the spinach thoroughly and discard any tough stems. Drain. Put the water into a large saucepan and bring to a brisk boil. Add the spinach and sugar and boil over high heat for 2 minutes.

2 Remove from the heat and rinse the spinach 3 times in cold water, then squeeze out the moisture using a bamboo mat (sudare) or by hand.

3 Sprinkle the spinach with the soy sauce and form it into a roll. Divide it into 2 pieces and set aside.

4 Break the eggs into a bowl, add the salt and stir with chopsticks until thoroughly blended but not foamy.

5 Gently heat a rectangular omelet pan (makiyaki-nabe), or an 8 inch skillet, and add just enough oil to coat the surface.

6 Pour half the egg mixture into the omelet pan and tilt the pan quickly so the egg covers the whole surface. When the egg is set and lightly browned on the underside, slide it out onto a bamboo mat (sudare) or a cloth.

7 Put one of the spinach rolls along the edge of the omelet and roll up the spinach in the omelet. Squeeze lightly to firm up the omelet roll.

8 Repeat the procedure with the remaining egg and spinach, then let the rolls cool. When cold, cut the rolls in 1 inch slices.

9 Transfer the spinach rolls to a serving platter and garnish with the radish waterlily, carrot feather, tomato rose and cucumber peel.

● As a variation, try a shrimp omelet. Pound 10 shelled shrimp to a paste and stir into the eggs, with a dash of sake. Mix 1 teaspoon arrowroot flour with 1 teaspoon water and stir into the egg mixture. Add all the egg mixture to the pan, cook until browned on the underside, then turn and brown the other side. Roll up in a bamboo mat (sudare) or thick cloth, let cool and slice.

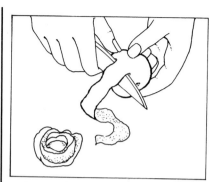

● To make a tomato skin rose, put a tomato in a bowl of boiling water for 1 minute. Drain and thinly pare off the skin, cutting in a spiral motion. Wind up the skin to form a rose shape.

● To make a radish waterlily for the garnish, make a series of small V-shaped cuts around the circumference of the radish. Pull the 2 halves apart then immerse in cold water for about 1 hour.

Egg bamboo
(*Takenoko-iri tamago-yaki*)

Preparation and cooking:
10 minutes

Serves 2-4
4 eggs
¼ teaspoon salt
¼ teaspoon freshly ground black pepper
2 teaspoons rice or cider vinegar
2 tablespoons vegetable oil
1 cup drained canned bamboo shoots cut in strips
1 teaspoon soy sauce
½ teaspoon sugar
1 teaspoon sesame oil
For garnish
1 scallion, minced

1 Beat the eggs in a bowl, then mix in the salt, pepper and vinegar.

2 Heat 1 tablespoon oil in a large skillet, add the bamboo shoots and stir-fry for 1 minute. Sprinkle with the soy sauce and sugar and stir-fry for a further 30 seconds.

3 Transfer the bamboo shoot mixture to a bowl and set aside. Heat the remaining oil in the pan and pour in the egg mixture.

4 Return the bamboo shoot mixture to the pan and stir into the egg. Cook over low heat, stirring, until the egg thickens.

5 Stir in the sesame oil, transfer to a warmed serving plate, garnish with minced scallion and serve at once.

Buckwheat omelets with vegetables
(*Udon-iri tamago-yaki*)

Preparation and cooking:
20 minutes

Serves 4
1 cup buckwheat meal
4 eggs, lightly beaten
½ cup water
1 tablespoon soy sauce
1 small onion, diced
1 green pepper, seeded and diced
1 cup sliced mushrooms
freshly ground black pepper
vegetable oil for cooking
For garnish
tomato wedges

1 Put the flour in a mixing bowl, add the eggs, water and soy sauce and beat to a smooth batter. Stir in the onion, green pepper and mushrooms. Season with black pepper to taste.

2 Heat a rectangular omelet pan (makiyaki-nabe) or an 8 inch skillet, and add just enough oil to coat the surface.

3 Pour half the egg mixture into the omelet pan and tilt the pan quickly so the egg covers the whole surface. When the egg is lightly browned on the underside, turn the omelet and cook on the other side. The vegetables should remain slightly crisp.

4 Slide the omelet onto a warmed serving plate and keep hot while cooking the remaining egg mixture in the same way.

5 Serve the omelets hot, garnished with tomato wedges.

● Buckwheat is a popular ingredient in Japan and in northern areas is sometimes used in place of rice. Buckwheat meal is commonly used to make noodles and here it is used to make omelets. Graham flour may be used instead.

Cucumber salad
(Age kyuri no sarada)

Preparation and cooking:
4½ hours

Serves 4
1 large cucumber
1 tablespoon salt
2 tablespoons sugar
1 sweet red pepper, seeded
4 thin slices of fresh gingerroot,
pared and cut in fine shreds
2 tablespoons sesame oil
¼ cup rice vinegar
1 tablespoon soy sauce

1 Cut the cucumber in half lengthwise and scoop out the seeds with a metal spoon. Cut each half in 1½ inch lengths, then slice each length into ¼ inch strips. Place in a colander, sprinkle with salt and half the sugar, then let stand for at least 15 minutes.

2 Meanwhile, cut the sweet red pepper into the same size strips as the cucumber. Rinse the cucumber strips under cold running water, drain and dry with a dish towel or absorbent kitchen paper.

3 Heat the oil in a skillet, add the cucumber and sweet red pepper strips, and the ginger shreds. Sauté over a high heat, stirring, for 2-3 minutes, or until the vegetables have slightly softened but are still crisp. Transfer them to a bowl.

4 Add the rice vinegar, the remaining sugar and the soy sauce to the vegetables. Toss until well coated. Transfer to a serving dish and leave to marinate for at least 4 hours in the refrigerator.

● This appetizer will keep in the refrigerator for 4-5 days. Use any leftovers as a relish with meat dishes.

Cucumber salad (Age kyuri no sarada)

Hot eggplant salad
(Age nasu no sarada)

Preparation and cooking:
1 hour

Serves 4
1 lb eggplants, thinly sliced
salt
2 tablespoons vegetable oil
Mustard dressing
1 teaspoon wasabi (Japanese
horseradish mustard), mixed to a
paste with water
2 tablespoons rice or cider vinegar
2 tablespoons soy sauce
1-2 teaspoons sugar
For garnish
sprigs of watercress

1 Make the dressing. Combine the wasabi, vinegar and soy sauce in a small mixing bowl. Add sugar to taste and stir until sugar has dissolved.

2 Arrange a layer of eggplant slices in a colander and sprinkle with salt. Continue layering and salting in this way until the slices are used up. Leave to drain for 30 minutes.

3 Rinse the eggplants under cold running water, drain and press out excess moisture. Pat dry with a cloth.

4 Heat the oil in a large skillet, add the eggplant slices and sauté until evenly browned on both sides.

5 Transfer to a warmed serving dish and pour over the mustard dressing. Garnish with watercress sprigs and serve at once.

Orange and white vinegared salad
(Namasu)

Preparation:
8 ¼ hours

Serves 4
½ lb daikon (Japanese white radish)
2 carrots
1 teaspoon salt
⅓ cup rice vinegar
1 teaspoon soy sauce
½ inch piece of fresh gingerroot, pared and chopped
1 tablespoon sugar

1 Peel the daikon and scrape the carrots; cut both vegetables into matchsticks about 1½ inches in length.

2 Put the daikon and carrots in a large mixing bowl and sprinkle with the salt. Leave for 30 minutes, then gather the mixture in both hands and gently squeeze out as much water as possible.

3 Combine the vinegar, soy sauce, ginger and sugar and pour the mixture over the vegetables. Stir to mix, then cover and leave in the refrigerator for about 8 hours.

● This salad will keep for up to 1 week, if stored in an airtight container in the refrigerator.

Chrysanthemum turnips
(Kikka-kabu)

Preparation:
4 hours

Serves 2
4 baby turnips
salt
⅓ cup rice vinegar
2 tablespoon superfine sugar
For garnish
½ sweet red pepper, seeded and cut in rings
grated rind of ½ lemon
shungiku (chrysanthemum leaves) or lettuce leaves

1 Cut the stems off the turnips and discard. Pare the turnips as thinly as possible.

2 Stand a turnip on its stem end and place a chopstick on each side of the base. Cut down the turnip, as though you were cutting the whole turnip in thin slices, but stop each stroke as the knife meets the chopsticks. Repeat across the other way to give a checkerboard effect.

3 Cover the cut turnips in salt water and let stand for about 30 minutes until soft.

4 Rinse the turnips, then pat dry on a clean cloth and stand in individual bowls.

5 Combine the vinegar, sugar and ¼ teaspoon salt and sprinkle the mixture over the turnips. Let stand for 3 hours.

6 Garnish the top of 2 turnips with sweet red pepper rings to represent red-centred chrysanthemums; then sprinkle grated lemon rind over the remaining turnips to represent yellow-centred chrysanthemums.

7 Stand the garnished turnips in a dish lined with chrysanthemum leaves to give a flower effect.

● Serve this salad as a side dish or as part of a salad spread.

Chinese cabbage with bonito flakes
(Hakusai no ohitashi)

Preparation and cooking:
30 minutes

Serves 4
8 Chinese cabbage leaves
salt
1 tablespoon rice vinegar
1 tablespoon soy sauce
¼ cup dashi (Japanese stock), see
page 10
For garnish
2 tablespoons katsuobushi (dried
bonito flakes)

1 Place cabbage leaves in a saucepan large enough to hold them comfortably and pour in enough boiling salted water to cover. Simmer, uncovered, for 5 minutes. Drain and arrange the leaves, one on top of the other, on a bamboo mat (sudare) or a heavy cloth napkin. Let cool.

2 Roll up the mat or cloth and squeeze gently to get rid of the excess moisture. Unroll and then re-roll the leaves tighter. Cut in 4 slices and set aside.

3 In a small bowl, combine the vinegar, soy sauce, stock and salt to taste. Mix well and pour over the cabbage. Garnish with the katsuobushi and serve.

● This is a popular Japanese winter vegetable dish.

Cold tofu
(Niyakko tofu)

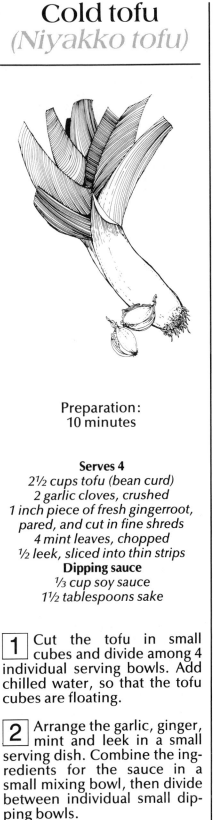

Preparation:
10 minutes

Serves 4
2½ cups tofu (bean curd)
2 garlic cloves, crushed
1 inch piece of fresh gingerroot,
pared, and cut in fine shreds
4 mint leaves, chopped
½ leek, sliced into thin strips
Dipping sauce
⅓ cup soy sauce
1½ tablespoons sake

1 Cut the tofu in small cubes and divide among 4 individual serving bowls. Add chilled water, so that the tofu cubes are floating.

2 Arrange the garlic, ginger, mint and leek in a small serving dish. Combine the ingredients for the sauce in a small mixing bowl, then divide between individual small dipping bowls.

3 To serve, each person sprinkles garlic, ginger, mint and leek to taste into the dipping sauce, then dips in the tofu cubes before eating.

Watercress and radish salad (Oranda garashi no sarada)

Watercress and radish salad
(Oranda garashi no sarada)

Preparation:
2¼ hours

Serves 4-6
2 bunches of watercress
1 bunch of red radishes
2 celery stalks, sliced
Soy dressing
⅓ cup vegetable oil
½ teaspoon sugar
2 tablespoons rice vinegar
1 tablespoon soy sauce
shichimi togarashi

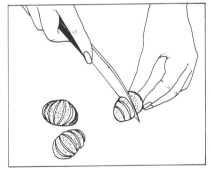

1 Wash and trim the watercress, discarding any yellow leaves. Dry thoroughly and chill, wrapped in a damp towel, in the refrigerator.

2 Wash and trim the radishes and cut across each radish, making thin slices almost through the radish. Drop them into a bowl of ice water and leave in the refrigerator for about 2 hours to open out into "accordions". Slice the celery.

3 To make the soy dressing, combine the oil, sugar, rice vinegar and soy sauce. Season to taste with shichimi togarashi.

4 Just before serving, place the watercress in a salad bowl; add the radishes and celery. Pour on the dressing and toss until every ingredient glistens.

Cucumber and wakame salad
(Kyuri to wakame no sumomi)

Preparation:
45 minutes

Serves 4
¼ lb wakame seaweed
1 cucumber, thinly sliced
¼ cup rice vinegar
2 tablespoons soy sauce
2 teaspoons sugar
½ teaspoon salt

1 Rinse the wakame and soak it in cold water for 20-30 minutes.

2 Drain the wakame and gently squeeze out the excess moisture. Cut in 1½ inch lengths.

3 Put the soaked wakame in a serving dish and mix in the cucumber.

4 Combine the vinegar, soy sauce, sugar and salt and pour the mixture over the vegetables. Serve at once.

Pickled turnip
(Kabu no tsukemono)

Preparation:
30 minutes, plus storing

Serves 4
1 large turnip, sliced paper thin
1 x 2 inch piece of kombu piece of seaweed
1½ inch piece of fresh gingerroot, pared and sliced
2 dry red chilies, chopped chopped rind of ½ lemon
½ carrot, cut in matchstick strips
2 teaspoons salt
Dressing
1 tablespoon mirin (sweet rice wine)
1 tablespoon soy sauce

1 Put the turnip, kombu seaweed, ginger, red chilies, lemon rind, carrot and salt onto a deep plate. Cover and place a heavy object, such as an iron, on top to compress the mixture. Leave for at least 12 hours.

2 To serve, remove the heavy object and uncover. Using your hands, gently squeeze any excess moisture from the pickle.

3 Transfer to a serving bowl and pour over the soy sauce and mirin. Toss gently to mix and serve at once.

Pickled red ginger
(Beni shoga)

Preparation and cooking:
3 hours

Makes 2½ cups
½ lb fresh gingerroot, pared and thinly sliced
1 tablespoon salt
2 cups rice or cider vinegar
⅔ cup sugar
½ teaspoon red food coloring

1 Cut the ginger slices in thin strips, 2 inches long, then place them in a shallow dish. Sprinkle the strips with the salt and let stand for 2 hours. Rinse the strips in cold water and drain.

2 Pour the vinegar into a heavy-bottomed saucepan and heat over medium heat. Add the sugar and stir until dissolved. Stir in the ginger strips, cover the saucepan and simmer gently for about 10 minutes.

3 Remove the pan from the heat, add the food coloring and stir to mix well. Let cool completely.

4 Pack the mixture into a sterilized pickling jar, cover and refrigerate. This preserved ginger will keep for about 1 year.

● To sterilize jars for pickling, wash and thoroughly rinse the jars, then stand on a rack or trivet in a large pan of water and bring to a boil. Remove from the pan, stand upside-down to drain, then put in a warm oven to dry out.

Spinach salad
(Horenso no sarada)

Preparation and cooking:
15 minutes

Serves 4
1 lb fresh spinach
Dressing
3 tablespoons sesame seeds, toasted and crushed
2 tablespoons soy sauce
1 tablespoons rice vinegar
1 teaspoon dry mustard
2 scallions, minced
2 teaspoons finely grated fresh gingerroot
½ teaspoon shichimi togarashi

1 Make the dressing. Combine all the dressing ingredients in a small serving bowl and mix to a smooth paste. Set aside.

2 Wash the spinach, discarding any tough stems. Put the spinach in a saucepan with only the water that clings to the leaves. Cover the pan and cook over medium heat for about 5 minutes until the spinach is soft and tender.

3 Drain the spinach well and gently press out as much moisture as possible using a bamboo mat (sudare) or your hands. Cut the pressed spinach into shreds about 2 inches long.

4 Transfer the spinach to a serving dish and serve at once, accompanied by the dressing.

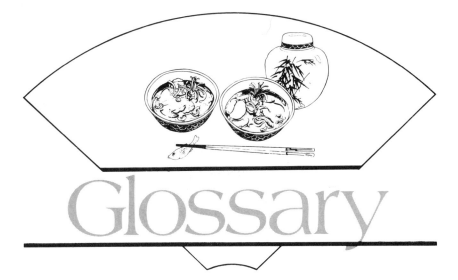

Glossary

Aburage	Deep-fried cakes of bean curd, sold plastic-wrapped or frozen. Plain bean curd can be used instead.
Azuki beans	Dried small red beans with a sweet taste.
Bamboo shoots	The young tender shoots of the tropical bamboo plant. Their crisp texture makes them a popular ingredient in vegetable dishes. Most widely sold in cans.
Chinese cabbage	Chinese cabbage looks like a pale Romaine lettuce and has a milder, more delicate flavour than Western cabbages. It is used raw in salads and cooked in vegetable dishes. The leaves are good for wrapping around fillings.
Daikon	A Japanese white radish which grows to 12 inches or more in length. It is milder than an ordinary radish. Icicle radishes or small sweet turnips make a fair substitute.
Ginger	Fresh gingerroot has a clean, pungent taste. A knobbly, lobed root, it is usually pared and then grated, cut into fine shreds or sliced. The Japanese eat it on its own, raw or pickled. Ginger is also used in marinades and sauces. Sold by weight, gingerroot should be hard with a smooth skin. Buy if from Oriental or Puerto Rican food markets.
Ginkgo nuts	The kernels of the maidenhair tree. They are sold canned and ready to use.
Kanpyo	Dried gourd strips used to flavor dishes or for tying around small bundles of seaweed.
Katsuobushi	Flakes of dried bonito fish, a member of the tuna family. One of the main ingredients of dashi, basic stock. Sold in bags and boxes.
Kombu	Dried kelp seaweed sold in long dried sheets which should only be wiped before using. Kombu is one of the two main ingredients of dashi, basic Japanese stock, but is also used as a flavoring and, when gently simmered, as a vegetable.
Konnyaku	Small gelatinous cakes processed from a vegetable known as devil's tongue. Sold canned or in small cartons.

Lotus root	A white sausage-shaped vegetable. Sliced thinly, it reveals its beautiful symmetrical pattern. Sold fresh or canned.
Mirin	A sweet rice wine used for cooking. Sherry can be substituted.
Miso	A naturally fermented soy bean paste widely used to make soups and as a flavoring. Sold in plastic packs.
Nori	Dried laver seaweed pressed into paper-thin sheets. Before use, nori is usually toasted, to bring out its full flavor. Commonly used as a wrapping around rice and as garnish. Sold in packages.
Sake	The national alcoholic drink of Japan. Sake is a mild-tasting but potent rice wine. It is obtainable by special order from most liquor stores or you may substitute pale dry sherry.
Sansho	Japanese pepper made from the seed pods of the prickly ash tree. It has a mild flavor and is used for seasoning.
Sesame seeds	Sesame seeds should be first lightly toasted in a dry pan to bring out their nutty flavor. They are sprinkled on dishes or pounded in a mortar and then used in marinades or sauces.
Shichimi togarashi	A blend of various spices and flavorings used as a seasoning, it ranges from mild to fairly hot. Paprika can be substituted.
Shiitake	Japanese tree mushrooms cultivated by injecting fungus into the soft barks of water-soaked tree trunks. Sold dried, they need about 20 minutes soaking. Chinese dried mushrooms are less expensive; fresh mushrooms can also be substituted.
Shirataki	Transparent noodles made from the starch produced from the root of a vegetable known as devil's tongue. Sold in cartons.
Shungiku	The edible leaves of the chrysanthemum plant. They impart a subtle fragrance to soups and other dishes. Spinach has a similar color and texture but is more strongly flavored.
Soba	Noodles made from buckwheat flour.
Somen	Thin wheat flour noodles. Vermicelli can be used instead.
Tofu	Tofu is made from soy beans and has a soft curd texture. Sold in slabs, it is cut into cubes before using. Store in the refrigerator covered with water for up to one week, but change the water regularly. Also available canned and in an instant powdered form.
Udon	Wheat flour noodles. Use spaghetti as a substitute.
Vinegar	The Japanese use a distilled rice wine that makes a slightly sweet vinegar. Mild white vinegar is a suitable substitute.
Wasabi	Japanese horseradish mustard sold in powder form. English dry mustard is a fair substitute.
Wakame	A dark green long curly seaweed. Cooked as a vegetable. Sold dried, it should be soaked for 10 to 15 minutes.

Index